TOGETHER
THE GREAT COLLABORATION

DAVE FERGUSON

AND

PATRICK O'CONNELL

Dedications

This book is dedicated to all the hard-working leaders of a burgeoning number of local, regional, national and global church planting networks. You are the pioneers that make it accessible for church leaders to plant more churches and more effectively do the work of Jesus together.

This book is also dedicated to the inspiring church planters, network leaders and movement leaders in NewThing who are relentlessly committed to being a catalyst for movements of multiplying churches. We love being on mission together!

Special Invitation

Please consider attending one of our Exponential 2020 events. Our goal is to help shape your paradigm for multiplication, inspire and encourage you to multiply, and equip you to turn ideas into action. In our 2020 conferences, we'll be focusing on what it takes to work together to pursue Kingdom collaboration.

2020 Theme: Together: Pursuing the Great Collaboration

Locations and dates: Our global conference, Exponential in Orlando, Florida, is a full-service event with thousands of attendees, 150+ speakers, 40+ tracks, and 150+ workshops. Our Exponential regional events are shorter and geographically based (translating to lower overall costs for large teams). Regionals bring the full "punch" of the national conferences' five main stage sessions without the breakout workshops.

2020 National Event
Exponential // Orlando, Florida // March 2-5, 2020

2020 Regional Events
Boise, ID
Exponential Español
Washington, D.C.
Southern California
Bay Area California
Chicago
Houston
New York City

≡XPONENTIAL

MARCH 2-5, 2020
ORLANDO, FL

JOSSY CHACKO

DAVE FERGUSON

OSCAR MURIU

DANIELLE
STRICKLAND

ANDY STANLEY

SANDRA STANLEY

EFREM SMITH

PETE SCAZZERO

TOGETHER

PURSUING THE GREAT COLLABORATION

REGIONAL TOUR STOPS

Boise, ID

Exponential Español

Washington D.C.

Southern CA

Bay Area, CA

Houston, TX

Chicago, IL

New York City

For more information and to register visit:

exponential.org/2020

new thing

You want to multiply
we want to help.

We want to help you reproduce more leaders and churches by giving you the tools and the plan you need.

MCP
Multiplying Church Practicum

LARN
Launching A Reproducing Network

CC
Catalyst Communities

"LARN was the help we needed to move from good intentions to actually planting churches. The program provides great, practical tools and core practices built on years of experience. This is a great tool to take the next step in becoming a reproducing church and to grow as a leader." **Egil Ellingsen. Norway.**

Learn what it takes to catalyze a movement of reproducing churches.

For more info go to **newthing.org** or email **info@newthing.org**.

Inside

Preface from Exponential

Since Exponential's launch in 2006, we have come alongside church leaders to inspire, challenge and equip them to multiply disciple makers. We are a community of activists who believes that church multiplication is the best way to carry out Jesus' Great Commission and expand God's Kingdom. We dream of movements of Level 5 multipliers mobilized with new scorecards, new values, and new mindsets into every corner of society.

To help awaken that dream, Exponential is helping churches engage in the multiplication conversation through assessment tools and simple frameworks, such as the Becoming 5 framework, which has become a powerful tool churches are using throughout the world today. Other Exponential frameworks include the 3DM framework (the three critical dimensions of multiplication); five practices of hero making; the BE-DO-GO framework for mobilizing people God's way; and others (see Appendix 4 in this book for more on Exponential frameworks).

In 2020, Exponential's theme is Together: Pursuing the Great Collaboration. The framework we're introducing (and is explored in this book) says that we are called to Go (The Great Commission, Matthew 28) in Love (The Great Commandment, Mark 12) and we're called to do both Together (what we're calling The Great Collaboration, John 17).

Too many church leaders are going it alone as they start new churches instead of working together. We desperately need Level 5 leaders to emerge who will intentionally come together to catalyze movements of Level 5 multiplying churches.

If we're going to make a difference and move the multiplication needle from now 7 percent of U.S. churches ever reproducing (Level 4) to a tipping point of greater than 16 percent (resulting in tens of thousands of eternities changed), we need to start with a new scorecard and paradigm for success.

And that change must start in the heart and practices of leaders who recognize the truth that the mission of God won't be fulfilled by a few churches or dynamic leaders—but rather, hundreds of thousands of churches coming alongside each other.

You're now part of this ongoing multiplication conversation. Our prayer is that you'll learn from Dave and Patrick's insights and be inspired to link arms with other leaders as together we flood the fullness of Jesus into a desperate world.

Foreword

As a "movement mentor" to Dave Ferguson and Patrick O'Connell, it has been an absolute privilege to be in some small way involved in the content of this book and the growing number of church planting networks in the Western world. It has been a particular joy to observe Dave and Patrick apply the various elements of movement thinking to NewThing (the rapidly growing church planting network they lead) with great impact, both domestically and globally.

While Dave and Patrick have in the past written about multiplication and hero making as critical elements in movements, the book in your hands now focuses on a very neglected aspect of organizing for movement through church planting networks. In writing this book, they are actually providing "proof of concept"—vividly showing us that movements are the most effective way to achieve genuine and transformational kingdom impact.

The benefits of networks are evident. Dave and Patrick don't just know this through research; but firsthand through NewThing, the church planting network they lead. It is now growing rapidly on five continents by organizing the church much closer to the way the New Testament church (and other transformational movements) organized. It is operating more like the kind of movement that Jesus intended for His Church and because of this, I believe Jesus is blessing their commitment to extend His mission.

But *why* are networks of churches a significant key to unlocking the power of movements? Well, partly because they maximize the potential for trans-local collaborative undertakings without the need for controlling, unwieldy and costly centralized organization. Part of the logic inherent in collaboration is the recognition that the world doesn't actually change one person at a time. Apart from that idea being unscalable, it's an individualistic myth.

Rather, the world changes as a broad coalition of relationships formed among people who have a common cause and vision of what's possible. Networking based on the kingdom of God relieves us from having to worry about developing a critical mass to start something from within a limited brand or organization. Instead, strategy and emphasis fall on fostering the critical connections through which genuine trans-local movement can take place. As a result, networks are the means by which the core idea and purpose of any movement spreads. Boom!

But there is more: networking also lies at the heart of innovation because it provides a context of learning—specialists in innovation have called this "the intersection." We don't need to convince large numbers of people within an organization (a church, for instance) to change; instead, we focus on our connection with kindred spirits. And it's through the interaction of these critical relationships that we will develop the new knowledge, practices, courage and commitment that lead to transformational movement.[1]

In articulating what they are actively learning and implementing on the mission field, Dave and Patrick are gifting the rest of us who must follow the path they're blazing. Listen closely and heed their challenge to join or even start a church planting network.

I, for one, am thankful to my two brothers and pioneers in the journey.

—Alan Hirsch, author and missiologist

CHAPTER 1

Better Together

BIG IDEA: By God's design, we are better together.

We are better together.

Changing the world is more than any one of us can do—*but* it's not more than all of us can do together.

You don't have to look much farther than Scripture to see this truth. The Bible is crystal clear. In fact, Jesus' words to Jewish and Gentile believers in Matthew's Gospel inform the big idea of this book: *"For where two or three come together in my name, I am there with them"* (Matt. 18:20). Jesus' message tells us that when we unify, collaborate and come together as believers, He is present in a qualitative different way than when we are all alone.

[handwritten margin note: Context is for discerning right and wrong in discipline]

We are better together. [handwritten: a cord of 3 strands is not easily broken]

Let me help you grasp this profound truth by asking a question: Are you better off being isolated and secluded for long periods of time; or are you better doing life with good friends and a regular routine of relating?

We are better together!

I love getting on a plane and traveling all over the world. I thoroughly enjoy the opportunity to see what God is doing through planting new churches in amazing places like Damoh, India, or Bergen, Norway. But if I'm traveling unaccompanied without my wife or family for long stretches of time, it's simply not good. If I'm on my own for too long, admittedly, I become more susceptible to depression and temptation. I start to lack discipline. It's what God told us in the very beginning: *"It is not good for the man to be alone"* (Gen. 2:18).

We are better together.

Frederick II Experiment

Back in the 13th century, the German King Frederick II conducted a diabolical experiment to discover what language children would naturally grow up speaking if never spoken to. He was sure it would be German. To him, that premise seemed obvious, and it just needed to be proven! So to prove it, King Frederick took babies from their mothers at birth and placed them in the care of nurses who were forbidden to speak in their presence. He also imposed a second equally cruel rule: the nurses were not allowed to touch the infants. They were instructed to leave them alone with no physical or emotional contact.

Due to a horrific response, Frederick had to cut his experiment short. The tragedy revealed something very significant regarding human nature. As you may have guessed, the babies never grew up to speak *any* language because they all died.

It was the Italian historian Salimbene di Adam, in 1248, who made this scientific observation about the infants in Frederick's inhumane study: "They could not live without petting." The babies literally died from a lack of human touch and being left all alone.

Wow!

Modern medicine calls this phenomenon, "failure to thrive." For some reason, we humans flourish when we're in the presence of others who love us—and we gradually die when left alone. In his best-selling book, *Love and Survival,* Dr. Dean Ornish presents study after study that loving relationships are the chief influence for mental, emotional and even physical health. He summarizes the unexpected message of the rapidly accumulating body of data: "Anything that promotes feelings of love and intimacy is healing; anything that promotes isolation, separation, loneliness, loss, hostility, anger, cynicism, depression, alienation, and related feelings often leads to suffering, disease and premature death."[2]

Through controlled studies like Ornish's and others', modern science is now proving that human beings are literally engineered for loving relationships. We are made for each other, and we need each other. It's as if our DNA contains the message, "We are better together."

What's Killing the Body of Christ?

If it's true that a lack of being together can physically kill a human body, could the same be true for the Church—that a lack of being together could kill the body of Christ? If isolation and loneliness can lead to suffering and premature death in a human body, could separation and alienation lead to sickness and fatality in Christ's body?

And while we're asking good questions, if the church is made of people who thrive in community and die on our own, does it make sense that the body of Christ will flourish when we come together and will perish when we abandon one another?

If it's true that a lack of being together can physically kill a human body, could the same be true for the Church?

I would respond to all four questions with a loud and emphatic, "Yes! We are better together."

For more than a generation, the church in the Western world has looked to the star pastor, the one charismatic leader, or the efforts of a fast-growing church to lead the way in helping us accomplish the mission of Jesus. I don't have to tell you it's not working. Not only is it not working, it's also producing isolation, separation, loneliness, anger, cynicism and depression as we try to do it all on our own.

Every available measurement of the Western church indicates that Christ's body on earth is not virile enough to reproduce or healthy enough to give birth. The church is suffering, diseased and on the verge of a premature death. What's killing the body of Christ?

We have forgotten that creation fact God Himself laid out for Adam: *"It is not good for the man to be alone"* (Gen. 2:18). And we have forgotten the spiritual reality that Jesus shared with us, *"For where two or three come together in my name, I am there I with them"* (Matt. 18:20). ? Not a great way to use this verse

Ultimately, we have forgotten this primal life-giving truth—we are better together!

BETTER TOGETHER

"Only through collaboration with other churches, church planters, church leaders and Christ followers is there any hope of seeing the Jesus mission accomplished. As networks have formed and reproduced, we have experienced more impact and fun then we could have ever imagined!" **—Troy McMahon, Kansas City NewThing Network**

Better Together

In the following pages, I want to start a conversation with you about how, by God's design, we are always better together. The "I" here is actually a "we" because this book is written by me (Dave Ferguson) and my co-author and NewThing Global Director Patrick O'Connell—because we, too, are better together! To make this book more readable, we've decided to keep it in my voice. But know that what I say is rooted in the work Patrick and other leaders have pioneered and championed.

I'll begin this important and needed conversation by showing you a huge problem in our efforts to accomplish the mission of Jesus. We have really missed something, and I can't wait to start this discussion in the next chapter. In the following chapters, you'll find a rich theological foundation for how God existed from the beginning of time in togetherness. My hope is this theological underpinning will help you understand that being made in the image of God means we are *always* better together.

In the second half of the book, this conversation about how you and I are better together dramatically expands as I show you tremendous macro implications of this big idea and challenge you to consider that *churches*—including your church—are also always better together. Make no mistake. I'm whole-heartedly challenging you to join or even start a church planting network. Why? Because the mission of Jesus and seeing a church planting multiplication movement won't be accomplished by a single individual, one charismatic leader or a solo church. His mission will be accomplished only when God's people and His Church come together, acknowledging Jesus as Lord—and then pursue His mission as their sole focus. When they commit to building His kingdom versus their castle. We are better together.

The mission of Jesus and seeing a church planting multiplication movement won't be accomplished by a single individual, one charismatic leader or a solo church.

You will notice throughout the book, we've included callouts labeled "Better Together" with words of encouragement and instructions straight from those who are leading church planting networks. These are leaders building the kingdom and not their own castle. You may also notice that there is an absence of women network leaders. I hope this is not a discouragement to female leaders, but instead a reminder of how much you are needed and that we would like to help. Ponder the wisdom of these network leaders and notice how all of them have come to the conclusion that we are better together.

BETTER TOGETHER

"No one plants a church alone. It takes pioneering leaders, sending churches, supporting churches, prayer partners, external overseers, internal volunteers and, of course, the work of God's Spirit. Church planting networks ensure that all parties work together to accomplish what no one group or individual could do on their own. And, when new churches become contributors in the network to plant even more the result is a multiplication movement and the possibility of exponential kingdom expansion." **—Brent Storms, Orchard Group**

I call this a conversation because I think this is just the beginning of some very important discoveries that could change the trajectory of the Western church and the spiritual landscape of where we call home. After you've read this book, I want to engage with you in this conversation. Email me at daveferguson@communitychristian.org or Patrick at patrickoconnell@newthing.org and let us know what you think. I want to hear it. Patrick wants to hear it. We both love talking about this biblical truth. I'm dreaming big about what could happen as we move forward together.

Let's get this conversation started with the next chapter. Keep reading. Over the next few pages, I'll unpack how I realized what we're missing as we pursue the mission of Jesus— and then explain how you and your church can be a part of seeing Jesus' mission accomplished.

CHAPTER 2

What's Missing From the Mission?

BIG IDEA: We accomplish the mission of
Jesus when we go and love together.

"There is a piece missing!"

Puzzles are one of my wife Sue's very favorite things! She likes crossword puzzles, logic puzzles, word searches, cryptograms and almost any other kind of puzzle. But her favorite is jigsaw puzzles. Every holiday, she asks me to set up the card table in the corner of our living room where she dumps out 1,000 puzzle pieces. While others in close proximity are hanging out, watching sports or snacking, she'll try to coax any of the other four family members into joining in and helping her solve the puzzle, one piece at a time.

This book is like that card table. And the puzzle is what we are calling the Jesus mission. I hope to coax you into joining me in this nine-chapter conversation about how we are better together. I believe it could be the missing piece!

Last Christmas, Sue and one of the kids had linked together almost all 1,000 puzzle pieces. With only a couple dozen pieces left, they were getting excited at completing this two-day effort.

"We're just about finished, come and look!" Sue said, calling in all the family to celebrate the culmination of this Christmas break accomplishment. The last ten pieces were much easier to find spots for than the first ten. As Sue put in the last piece, she paused … and then yelled, "No!" In frustration, she grumbled, "There's a piece missing!"

So, the search began…

Searching For Level 5 Multiplying Churches

For an entire generation, the Western church has been on a search trying to solve this puzzle of what it takes to create movement and accomplish the mission of Jesus. I have been a part of this search. The fact that you're reading this book tells me you have also been part of this search.

Research has conclusively shown that a church planting movement is the best way to reach people with the Good News of Jesus. We know that new churches will typically see three to four times as many conversions as established churches ten years of age or older. But while we know it, we're not doing enough about it!

What we need are Level 5 churches! Not familiar with Level 5 multiplying church terminology? Let me explain it or give you a refresher based on our latest research. Exponential partnered with LifeWay Research to study churches across the United States. Every church falls into Level 1, Level 2 or Level 3. Here's a quick explanation of each level

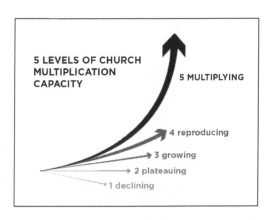

5 LEVELS OF CHURCH MULTIPLICATION CAPACITY

5 MULTIPLYING

4 reproducing

3 growing

2 plateauing

1 declining

(for more on this multiplication framework, check out the free Exponential eBook, *Becoming a Level 5 Multiplying Church*). Here's a brief breakdown:

> *Level 1: Subtraction, scarcity and survival.* Level 1 churches are experiencing some combination of declining attendance, staffing, income and conversions. Without a turnaround, Level 1 churches eventually die, usually in the short-term.

> *Level 2: Plateaued, seeking the next catalyst to spark a season of growth.* Level 2 churches experience some combination of flat attendance, staffing, income and conversions. These churches may see temporary ups and downs, but their overall trend is flat.

> *Level 3: Addition, growth and expansion of impact.* Level 3 churches have a strong growth culture with some combination of increasing attendance, staffing, income and baptisms. Leadership development and conquering the next growth barriers are often key priorities.[3]

Research revealed that thirty-five percent of U.S. churches are subtracting (Level 1); thirty-five percent are plateauing (Level 2); and thirty percent are adding (Level 3). Every church has a culture that can be placed in one of these three levels. Every church is subtracting, plateauing or growing.

For an entire generation, the Western church has been on a search trying to solve this puzzle of what it takes to create movement and accomplish the mission of Jesus.

You can compare churches' life cycles to the human life cycle: birth, development, growth, decline and death. But also in that mix is reproduction. In the same way that people can have children and grandchildren, churches can also reproduce through church planting and give life to multiple generations of new churches. Exponential's framework adds clarity to the possibility of reproducing by explaining that churches can also be Level 4 or Level 5. Here's what that looks like:

> *Level 4: Make starting new churches a priority.* Their approach to starting new churches is strongly programmatic; beyond simply adding to their number, reproduction has become an important part of their strategy.
>
> *Level 5: Multiply, release and send out everyday missionaries and church planters.* Reproduction is so deeply embedded in the DNA of Level 5 churches that they would need a strategy to stop it from happening. These churches are deeply committed to biblical disciple making—disciples who make disciples, who plant churches that plant churches, to the fourth generation. This commitment results in networks of reproducing churches that reach non-Christians at a much higher rate of conversion than other churches.

A couple years ago, research showed only four percent of U.S. churches were reproducing. In light of that finding, at Exponential we launched what we call the "4 to 10 mission"—to see the needle move from four percent to ten percent of churches reproducing within this generation. We dreamed of seeing multiplication becoming the primary metric for success in churches.

BETTER TOGETHER

"When Jesus comes back, He's not coming for a harem; He's coming for His Bride. We are one church—His church—and for that reason alone we should collaborate with other churches to accomplish the Jesus mission." —**Dave Dummitt, West Michigan/Detroit NewThing Network**

That's where this new study comes in: to determine if the needle is actually moving in Level 1, 2 and 3 churches, and to understand the current rate of reproduction (Level 4) and multiplication (Level 5) in U.S. churches. I'm excited to tell you that the new research reveals evidence that God's hand is definitely moving. The number of Level 4 reproducing churches has grown from four percent to seven percent.

While this may seem like a small change, consider this. Every one percent increase makes a profound and lasting impact that continues multiplying itself forward. Each one percent increase in Level 4 reproducing churches represents approximately 3,000 churches committed to reproducing new churches. And the result is millions of additional people finding their way back to God.

If we're going to see a movement and the mission of Jesus accomplished, then more churches must reproduce new churches, send out leaders, and create a culture of multiplication. I would love to see every church in the United States become a Level 4 or Level 5 church. If we can get that number to ten percent or sixteen percent, the United States will never be the same!

And while it's very encouraging that we are seeing an increase in Level 4 reproducing churches, the question remains: why aren't we seeing more Level 5 multiplying churches? And why are there no church planting movements in the West. That is our pursuit!

For me, the hunt for a movement and Level 5 multiplication started when we planted Community Christian Church in Chicago. That pursuit continues today, now as a lead pastor who has seen that church grow very large and into multiple locations.. I've had a unique vantage point from which to pursue this exploration as the visionary leader for NewThing, a global organization of reproducing churches with more than 155 networks and over 2,500 churches committed to reproducing. And as the president of the Exponential conference, I've had the privilege of meeting and talking with many of you and hearing about your own pursuit of putting together the puzzle pieces.

If we're going to see the mission of Jesus accomplished, then more churches must reproduce new churches, send out leaders, and create a culture of multiplication.

The Great Commission: GO

Let me start at the beginning, back when I was finishing up undergrad studies in preparation to plant a church. During that time, the Charles E. Fuller Institute for Evangelism and Church Growth profoundly influenced me. I took every course I could; ordered every resource they made available; and listened to every cassette tape I could (yep, all pre-digital era!). Over and over, leaders like Donald McGavaran, Carl George, C. Peter Wagner and others would challenge us to fulfill the Great Commission:

"Therefore go and make disciples of all nations, baptizing them in the name of the Father and of the Son and of the Holy Spirit, and teaching

them to obey everything I have commanded you. And surely I am with you always, to the very end of the age" (Matt. 28:19-20).

For most of us in that era, when we thought of Christ and His mission, the first thing that came to mind were these verses. In a word, that passage could be summarized as "Go!" And we were all for that (still are). We believed that we had to go and take the Good News of the gospel to all people.

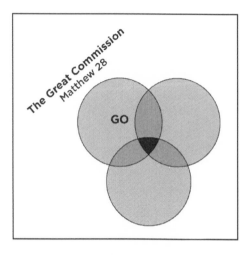

I was so gung-ho in college, I started something called the "Soul Winners Club." I'm embarrassed to admit it, but I harassed every fellow student and shamed every faculty member into joining me in doing street evangelism or going door-to-door to present the gospel. Why? Because we are supposed to Go! So I was going to go and if I had to go, I was going to make sure everyone else was going with me! Yes, a few people came to faith, but a lot more believers were alienated by my overzealous and misguided efforts.

About that same time, two young pastors planted innovative and evangelistic-oriented new churches. One was in the northwest suburbs of Chicago and the other in sunny Southern California. Both were introducing unique evangelistic strategies and zealously reminded us that "lost people matter to God." Rick Warren and Bill Hybels helped restore the priority of evangelism; many of us leaned into it and learned from them.

So when we planted Community Christian Church, we also leaned in and listened closely to both leaders. They were modeling for us a new way to "Go" and fulfill the Great Commission. We took what we learned from them, added our own unique passion and took on the mission of "helping people find their way back to God." Over the years, we saw thousands of people come to faith and we advanced the mission in our community. But when it came to the impact the big "C" church was making in our city or the United States, we were falling farther and farther behind.

Just consider some of these sobering and sad statistics: According to a recent Gallup poll, the number of adults in the United States that attend religious services weekly or almost weekly has declined ten percent in the last decade from forty-eight percent in 2008 to thirty-eight percent in 2018. According to the Pew Research Center, the number of people identifying as "nones" (no religious affiliation at all) has increased by seven percent from sixteen percent in 2005 to twenty-three percent in 2015. This is a serious missional problem for the Church! Even though we were doing our best to full the Great Commission, something was definitely still missing!

So the search continued…

BETTER TOGETHER

"Church planting networks provide a way for everyone to get involved in church planting. When local churches band together relationally and financially they can, typically, do what no one church could do in serving as a launching pad from which new churches to take off."
—Justin Moxley, Stadia

The Great Commandment: LOVE

It was about that time that multiple voices from a variety of places in North America and around the world began to identify the missing missional piece: "We need to not only fulfill the Great Commission, but also the Great Commandment." They would cite Mark 12:30-31:

Love the Lord your God with all your heart and with all your soul and with all your mind and with all your strength. The second is this: 'Love your neighbor as yourself.'

Then came the challenge: "If we focus only on going into the world, but not loving our world, the mission of Jesus will never be accomplished."

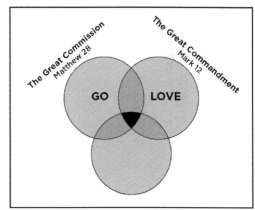

Within a few months, Steve Sjogren wrote *Conspiracy of Kindness: A Unique Approach to Sharing the Love of Jesus"* (2008); Hugh Halter and Matt Smay released *The Tangible Kingdom: Creating Incarnational Community"* (2008); and Alan Hirsch published *The Forgotten Ways: Reactivating the Missional Church* (2009). Each thought leader placed a high value on the Great Commission but challenged us to go about it in a way that prioritized the Great Commandment of loving the people in our communities and neighborhoods just like Jesus does.

At the same time, a generation of Millennials were coming into church leadership; they seemed to intuitively understand this integration of both "going" and "loving." When they were asked about tangible ways to love their community through volunteerism and service, 50 percent more Millennials said it was "very important" versus the previous generation.

At this point, new and old churches began to put into place this missing piece of practical and tangible expressions of love. More and more churches partnered with local schools to do mentoring, service projects and Christmas outreaches. Churches and their small groups or missional communities placed a new emphasis on neighboring and relational strategies to love the people and places where you live. Churches mobilized their people to live out the Great Commandment.

Yes, love was a missing piece to the missional puzzle. This brought a much-needed awakening that we couldn't just go and win souls; we needed to love the whole person and their community. But the church in the West was still not seeing movement. The mission was not being accomplished. As I mentioned earlier, only four percent (Level 4) of all churches in the United States were reproducing new churches, and less than a handful were multiplying several generations of new churches (Level 5).

So the search continued…

The Great Collaboration: TOGETHER

On a trip to Europe a few years ago, I got a glimpse of what I believe is the missing piece. I was invited to speak at a gathering called NC2P (National Church Planting Process) in Berlin, Germany. When I walked into the large meeting room, I saw twenty-seven round tables with six to eight leaders sitting at each table. Quickly, I asked my host who was in the room.

"Those are twenty-seven cross-denominational teams from every country in the European Union," he explained.

I wanted confirmation: "These are leaders from different denominations all working together?"

"Yes," my host assured me. "They are each collaborating together on a church planting strategy to reach their country."

I wasn't sure I believed him. So, I started walking around the room introducing myself and asking them who they were and their denomination. He was right—Reformed working alongside Armenians; people who were complementarian strategizing with egalitarians; Pentecostals working with Baptists. Each team had committed to a three-year process with the vision of a church planting movement across all of Europe. It was one of the most remarkable gatherings I've ever witnessed! This diverse group of churches and leaders coming together and collaborating to plant more churches set the stage for a movement of multiplying churches.

This was the missing piece!

I was at a NewThing North American huddle of network leaders when I began to understand what we're missing. NewThing Global Director (and my collaborator on this book) Patrick O'Connell was laying out a theological framework for why we needed to create networks and why networks were so important to creating movement and accomplishing the mission of Jesus.

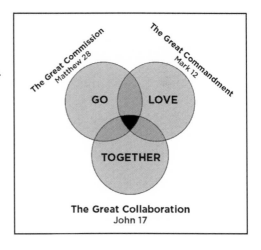

What Patrick was about to say was absolutely profound and would help me clearly understand the missing piece of movement and the Jesus mission.

I later found out that Patrick had really struggled to put together this message. Here's how he describes it playing out…

"I was preparing my message for our NewThing North American Huddle. I had been asked to talk about movements in North America and what we could do to see more of them.

What was I going to say to these leaders? After all, we don't see any church planting movements in the United States. Yet, I lead a global organization dedicated to helping start movements? #conundrum

A couple of days went by and after some prayer and journaling, I still didn't have an answer. The Huddle was fast approaching. My lack of an answer was really starting to bother me. *Maybe there wasn't an answer?*, I thought. It seemed like I would have nothing meaningful to offer these leaders.

So I read chapters of some key text on mission. (Thank goodness for Kindle.) I talked to a few leaders from other contexts but still didn't have any unique or interesting insight.

Feeling a bit desperate, I had a thought: *I should read through the Gospels and review what Jesus said about His movement and how Christ-followers were going to accomplish it.* (Good idea, right?) I read all four Gospels straight through. Then, I read each one a second time. That's when I saw it. While Jesus says much about His mission, three "Greats" stood out to me—one I never noticed before.

Jesus gives us three commands about His mission. From my Army days, I understand commands. A command is, well, to be obeyed. It's not optional. While there is always much more we can learn from Jesus about His kingdom, there are three essential commands: The Great Commission (Matthew 28); The Great Commandment (Mark 12) *and* the Great Collaboration (John 17)—the one we had omitted.

Could it be that we had forgotten (or perhaps ignored) a critical component of the Jesus mission? Could it be that we were refusing to abide by one of Jesus' commands and, as a result, had stymied our effectiveness when it comes to church planting?

As followers of Jesus, we must listen and obey Jesus' commands if we expect to accomplish His mission. I drew the three "Greats" of the mission as a Venn diagram (see above). That was the plan Jesus gave His Church to accomplish His mission! Then I knew what I would say to those NewThing leaders."

As Patrick started talking that day, I remember sitting back in my chair, smugly telling myself, *I've heard all this before.* He drew the first circle and explained the Great Commission. Then he drew a second circle, adding the Great Commandment. But as he drew a third circle, he said, "Right before Jesus left planet Earth, He reminds His closest followers of His vision for how the mission would be accomplished and gave us this third 'great' in John 17:22-23: *"…that they may be one as we are one— I in them and you in me—so that they may be brought to complete unity. Then the world will know you sent me and have loved them even as you have loved me…"* Then Patrick finished, "This is the Great Collaboration! Yes, we are to go, yes, we are to love! But here's what I believe is the missing piece from the mission: we are to go … and love … but together!"

If the church of Jesus Christ could put all three of these pieces together—Go-Love-Together—we could realize the dream of the kingdom of God!

Jesus' Mission

Now Patrick had my full attention as he drew a Venn diagram and said with full-throated confidence, "We must obey all three of these commands: The Great Commission – Go. The Great Commandment – Love. The Great Collaboration – Together. It's when we put all three of these together—and *only* when we put all three of these together—that we'll accomplish the Jesus Mission! It's us doing this together … that is what is missing!"

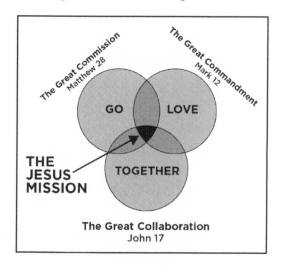

If the mission of Jesus and movement making was a puzzle, Patrick was showing us the missing piece. I felt a rush of conviction as I took it all in! If the church of Jesus Christ could put all three of these pieces together—Go-Love-Together—we could realize the dream of the kingdom of God!

How to Plant 100,000 Churches

I vividly remember the day I looked at my schedule and saw I had an appointment with a guy named Sam Stephens. Not knowing who he was, I asked my assistant Pat about him.

"I thought *you* knew him," she said. "All I know is that he's from India."

I went into the meeting not knowing anything about this guy. But I put on a happy face, extended my hand and asked him to tell me his story. Sam began by telling me how in the 1960s his father had started a mission to plant churches in India and that by 1992, there were 200 churches. Wow! 200 churches. Now he had my attention.

Sam is a super-humble guy, so I had to drag the details out of him. He went on to explain, "In 1992, I took over the mission and we began to insist on two things:

1. That every church planter would not only plant a church but also have an apprentice church planter—someone who would come alongside them and learn how to plant a church so we could reproduce every year.
2. That as we grew, every church planter would be in a network to encourage and support them in doing what they said they wanted to do—to reproduce a new church every year!"

Now I was really curious. "How is it going?" I asked.

He casually replied, "Well, we now have 70,000 churches." I'm glad I was sitting down. This was incredible. "How many people does that represent?" I asked. His reply took my breath away: "I think about 3.5 million," he said. Then he added, "But we are praying for 100,000 new churches that reach 5 million people!"

How did this kind of multiplication happen? From my perspective, each church planter was committed to being a hero maker. Not only did they lead their church, they also apprenticed a church planter every year and sent them out to plant a church. To keep people encouraged and accountable, Sam put every leader into small networks. These networks would meet together once a month for training, a meal and accountability around the goals they set together.

What Sam told me next, I will never forget (and one of the reasons why we asked him to write our afterword for this book): *"Churches working together in networks are the backbone of movement."* Networks are the missing piece of the Great Collaboration! This is how leaders and churches can do this together!

"Churches working together in networks are the backbone of movement." –Sam Stephens, India Gospel League

---

Go–Love–Together—But Where Do You Start?

When I saw Patrick draw those three circles and when I heard Sam tell me his story of planting 100,000 churches by using small networks, I got an adrenaline rush at the possibility of fully understanding what it takes to accomplish the mission of Jesus. Putting together all three pieces: the Great Commission, the Great Commandment and the Great Collaboration—Go-Love-Together—felt like finally solving the puzzle. Wow! Maybe movement *is* possible.

My hunch is that right now you're feeling the same kind of excitement I did when I put these missing pieces together. But you're also probably feeling equally overwhelmed. Maybe you're thinking…

> *…but I'm still working on getting an apprentice.*
> *…but I'm just trying to get this one church started!*
> *…but I'm still working on getting my people to go and love.*
> *…who am I to start a network?*

Don't panic. Don't give up. Just keep reading. Launching your own network is probably not the place to start. It might be what God calls you to do in time. But before you're ready to join or start a network, you must first understand Jesus' vision for the Great Collaboration and what it fully means that we are better together.

Over the next few chapters, this simple diagram of concentric circles will serve as a guide to help you fully understand the Great

Collaboration and its individual elements. It starts with being together with God.

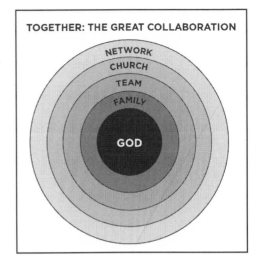

TOGETHER: THE GREAT COLLABORATION

NETWORK
CHURCH
TEAM
FAMILY
GOD

Together With God

The Great Collaboration starts with being together with God. Before God creates community *through* you, He must first be in community *with* you. Only a whole and healthy leader who lives in communion with God can lead their family, team and church into greater experiences of being together with God and one another.

Together as a Family

The Great Collaboration starts with intimacy between you and God and then is lived out in an intimate marriage and healthy family. The family is the first priority of the Jesus mission and never a distraction from difference making.

Together as a Team

The mission of Jesus and becoming Level 5 multiplying churches cannot be accomplished by a single individual or one charismatic leader. The Great Collaboration asks us to come together as teams made up of people with unique gifts and callings to equip and mobilize all of God's people for mission.

Together as a Church

Living in togetherness is always a part of following Jesus. It wasn't optional for Jesus. It wasn't optional for the first apostles. It wasn't optional for the first Christians and it's not optional for us! The church was designed to be God's eternal community where we experience reconciliation with Him and with others. Too many church leaders are leading churches but are not really a part of those churches. For us to fulfill the Great Collaboration we must be church leaders who live in togetherness and lead in togetherness with our churches.

Together as a Network

When churches come together to form networks, they're obeying Jesus' command of the Great Collaboration and discovering the missing piece of movement. Networks who have a sole focus on planting new churches are a powerful force. But for these networks to be effective, it requires leaders and churches coming together in unity to solve the puzzle and build God's kingdom instead of creating their own individual castles.

So let's continue this conversation by turning the page and discovering *what to do* but first *why to do it.* You are about to discover that the Great Collaboration is not another innovative church growth idea to try. It is a universal theological truth that's older than time itself. Intrigued?

CHAPTER 3

Together with God

BIG IDEA: The Great Collaboration starts
with being together with God.

God Himself is better together.

This is a simple, yet crucial theological truth. It explains *why* the
Great Collaboration is so important. It also explains *why* we are better
together. Let me say it again so that it sinks in: *God Himself is better
together.*

Not sure what I mean?

Stick with me. This chapter is vitally important to our conversation.
For the next several paragraphs, I'm going to do a deep theological
and missiological dive. I call it conjuring up my inner Alan Hirsch. ☺
When Alan writes something, you always have to read it twice. But
then it's ten times as good. (If you've read *The Forgotten Ways* or any of
Alan's other books, you know what I'm talking about.)

I remember when I co-authored *On the Verge* with Alan. He would
always challenge me, "Dave, we need to make sure this book is
robust!" So, the next few sections are robust! Most of this came
from people smarter than me who influenced my understanding of a
relational God. One was Kansas City church planter Tim Southerland

when we co-taught a series at Community Christian Church titled, "The Theory of Everything." Much of the following comes from him. Make sure you're fully caffeinated—you may need it. But read every word and if necessary, read it slowly. This will give you the theological foundation for the Great Collaboration and also further explain why we are better together.

Ready. Deep breath. Here we go…

God Who Exists in Togetherness

At the very start of Scripture—literally the first verse of Genesis—we're told that the God who created us and in whose image we are created has existed in togetherness from the beginning of time. And that this same God who has always existed in togetherness invites us to do life together with Him. To understand better, let's go back to the very beginning…

We see the "togetherness" in the first three verses of Genesis:

> **Genesis 1:1 –** *In the beginning was God …*
> Genesis was originally written in Hebrew, and the word used for God is *Elohim*, a grammatically plural noun. Why is it plural?

> **Genesis 1:2 –** *…the Spirit of God was hovering over the waters …*
> In the next verse, Scripture tells us that the Spirit of Elohim is hovering over the face of the waters. So Elohim also has a Spirit.

> **Genesis 1:3 –** *And God said …*
> Then in verse 3, Elohim speaks and we see that Elohim has words.

Throughout the rest of the chapter, God creates. And everything that God, the Spirit of God and the Word of God create is "good." The light was good. The sky and ocean and land are good. The fish and swimming creatures are good. The birds and flying creatures are good. It's all good!

And then God reveals more of Himself to us…

> **Genesis 1:26 – *Then God said, "Let us make mankind in our image, in our likeness …"***

"Us?"

"Our?"

That may sound weird to us, but like I told you, the "us" and "our" fit because the word Elohim is plural. But Elohim doesn't mean "Gods" because the verb tenses and adjectives that refer to Elohim are all singular, referring to one being.

Genesis 1 isn't the only place in Scripture where we see this; we also find it in John 1:1: *In the beginning* (sound familiar?) *was the Word…"* Remember that in Genesis 1 God speaks and in John 1 we learn, *In the beginning was the Word and the Word was with God and the Word was God.*

This Word is not an it; the Word in these scriptures is a He. We see that in the next three verses of John 1: *He was with God in the beginning, through Him all things were made, without Him nothing was made that has been made. In Him was life, and that life was the light of all people …* Then a few verses later: *… And the Word became flesh and dwelt among us …* This Word that was with God and was God from the beginning becomes a human being, dwells among us and took on the name of Jesus.

God who created us and in whose image we are created has existed in togetherness from the beginning of time.

God has existed from the beginning as one and yet three. As soon as I say that, the mathematician inside you starts thinking, *That's not possible!* Before you get stuck on how it doesn't add up, please get what these scriptures are telling us about God: Though God is one, He has always existed in togetherness; and it was in togetherness that He created a perfect world.

While we absolutely need to understand our triune God, we also need to understand how God related in togetherness. For this key understanding, let's go back to the Gospel of John, beginning with 16:14, which tells us that the Spirit glorifies the Son. A few verses later, John 17:4 says the Son glorifies the Father. And in the next verse, John tells us the Father glorifies the Son and that this glorifying has been going on for all eternity.

To "glorify" something or someone means to praise, enjoy, to direct attention to them, and most of all to delight in them. To glorify someone, you must serve or defer to him or her. So from all eternity, before the beginning, the Father, Son and Spirit have been glorifying each other. They have this un-self-centered relationship in which they revolve around each other. None makes the others revolve around himself. Instead, each person in the Trinity loves, adores, defers to, and rejoices in the others. That gives us a beautiful picture: God existing in a community of persons who know and love each other. Throughout all eternity, their relationship is this dynamic, pulsating, dance of joy and love.

Some of the earliest Christ-followers had a word for this dance. They called it "perichoresis." It comes from the same Greek word that gives us the word "choreography." Perichoresis means to dance or flow around each other. My wife says my dancing looks like I'm in a boxing match (don't think of that kind of dancing). Instead, imagine a beautiful dance of endless, creative, self-giving love where the other dancers are drawing the attention away from themselves toward the other. Can you see it? The trinity explains why we believe that "God is love." (I John 4:8).

This is so, so important! Because when God says, ...*let us make man in our own image* in Genesis 1, He tells us that we are to be a reflection, an image of who He is. Just as the God of the universe is a dance of love, our lives are also meant to join in that dance of self-giving love. Our creator tells us you were made to live together in love and to be loved. Living in love together is not just an important *part* of our life; it's meant to actually *be* our life and to bring life!

> Living in love together is not just an important *part* of our life; it's meant to actually *be* our life and to bring life!

Dancing Together With God

Several years ago, I had the privilege of attending a spiritual retreat led by author Brennan Manning. He was a brilliant writer and speaker. The retreat was very simple, but life- changing. Manning would speak, and then he asked us to go off by ourselves and journal about what we were experiencing with God. After being on our own, we came back and sat in groups to share our experiences.

He told a story from one summer retreat in Iowa City. A nun named Christine was one of the participants and when it was time for her to share in her group what she'd experienced, she said, "I got nothing. I'm not hearing anything. I'm not feeling anything. I must be doing something wrong." Manning had a way of comforting people. He quickly assured her, "No, no, no, it's ok, it's just different for you, it'll come." They went through the whole weekend. Each time when it was her turn to share, she'd say, "I got nothing."

Then the last day he spoke and everybody went off to journal. But this time, Christine had something.

"I don't know how to explain it," she shared. "It was like a dream. I was asking God to show me and help me understand what I'm missing; and suddenly it was like I was transported into this huge dance hall. It was like a ballroom, and everybody was dressed very elegantly. All around me, everyone was dancing, beautiful dances, perfectly, nobody missing a single step. I went over and stood against the wall. I stood there through a couple of songs all by myself. Then this gentleman came up to me. I don't know if he'd been there all along, but he had on this striking black tux with a red flower. He came up to me, extended his hand and said, 'Can we dance?' I told him, 'I'm not very good,' and he said, 'It's ok. I'll lead the way.'

"Next, he took me by the hand out on the dance floor and we began to dance. And I've never danced like that. We spun. We dipped. It was amazing. As we danced, everyone else stopped dancing and just formed a big circle around us. When the song ended, everyone applauded just for us. And the man looked at me and said, 'Thank you for having this dance with me.' As he looked into my eyes, I knew it was Jesus. Again he said, 'Thank you for this dance.' And then added, 'Let me tell you one more thing.' He bent down and whispered in my ear, 'Christine, I'm wild about you.'"

Christine concluded, "I know it sounds odd, but it's true. He said to me, 'I'm wild about you,' and I know I will never be the same again."

Together Take-Aways

I love that story! And when I heard Brennan Manning tell it in person … wow! I hope you took away from the theological deep dive and Manning's story that God is extending His hand to you, asking you to do life together with Him.

Let's pause to clearly restate what we're learning so far in this chapter:

1. God exists in a community of togetherness.
2. God creates in a community of togetherness.
3. God in Christ invites you to be together with Him.
4. God in Christ invites you to create together with Him.

I believe all of the above to be true; but my tendency is to do it on my own. My tendency is to depend on me. My tendency is to give *me* the credit.

That tendency is sin.

Our tendency is to gravitate away from God and away from others and to do what we want, when we want, on our own. We tend to worship ourselves, not God. We tend to point to ourselves, not God.

That tendency is sin.

That sinful tendency ruins what God wants to do in me and through me. And in you and through you.

> God is extending His hand to you, asking
> you to do life together with Him.

Pointing to Jesus

My co-author on this book, Patrick O'Connell, has a spiritual discipline of starting each day by looking at this painting titled *The Crucifixion* by the 15th-century artist Matthias Grünewald. In this masterpiece, John the Baptist stands to the left of the cross, holding an open book and pointing at the crucified Christ. In the background are

John the Baptist's words in Latin, "He must increase, but I must decrease."

Patrick had read that theologian Karl Barth kept a reproduction of *The Crucifixion* in his study to remind himself on a daily basis that his role was to point to Christ and His sacrifice on the cross. Inspired by that story, Patrick makes sure one of his first sights every morning is this  masterpiece and then he makes it his prayer that everything he does that day would point to Jesus.

To look at Grünewald's *Crucifixion* is a great daily discipline because this is a very real choice that each of us must make every day! We have to decide…

> …will this be a day that points to me or points to Jesus?

> …are my waking hours about doing my thing or God's thing?

> …will I work the next twenty-four hours to build my castle or God's Kingdom?

> …is this a day that will make much of me or much of Christ?

As leaders, we're called to face the crucified Christ and wrestle with these questions every day. Why? Because we're not prepared to lead a church, a team, our family or even ourselves until we're ready to point to Jesus and live life together with Him. It's just how you and I were created!

Please hear what I'm going to say next! The reason that shocking moral failures occur, large ministries collapse and movements implode always come back to this—a leader, leaders or leadership who wake up one day and rather than pointing to Christ, they point to themselves!

I'm not going to name names. We all have our own examples that break our hearts and have let us down. So you insert the name of your friend, pastor or high-profile leader who was making a huge kingdom impact and is now sitting on the sidelines or hasn't been heard from since. Go ahead; actually bring a name, a face, a person to mind. Got it? If you don't want that to be you, then, like Grünewald reminds us in his masterpiece, you must determine to wake up every day and point to Jesus!

> We're not prepared to lead a church, a team, our family or even ourselves until we're ready to point to Jesus and live life together with Him.

200 Locations *or* 200 Churches?

It was just a few years after planting Community Christian Church that God gave us a vision and an opportunity to go to multiple locations. Two friends of mine who were real estate developers had joined my small group in a serious spiritual search. Over the next twelve months, both them and their wives found their way back to God, and I had the privilege of baptizing each of them.

They were opening a new giant housing community in a Chicago suburb complete with a gym, fitness center, pool and all the extras. They had the idea that we should start another location of Community Christian in that neighborhood and they would design the gym and facilities to meet our requirements. It was a God thing! When we opened the second location, we had more than 500 people show up on the first Sunday. Not long after, a 153-year-old church gave us their facility. We closed it down, did some rehab and reopened it up six months later as a new location. The first Sunday, we had more than 600 people and standing room only in a little building that hadn't seen fifty people in years. Another God thing!

Going multi-site felt like we were on to something. And we were. Over the next few years, we started several more sites of Community Christian Church and continued to grow. It was then that I began to dream of 200 locations of our church. In my sanctified imagination, I could clearly see how we could grow this church to more than 100,000 people with 200 locations.

In the coming years, we added several more locations. But in the process, we also had to shut down or relocate some sites. At that point, a church in 200 locations wasn't quite as easy as it seemed at first. But I continued to cast a vision for a church that could get to 200 locations across Chicagoland.

BETTER TOGETHER

"Our willingness to work together in love not only makes the gospel more believable to an unbelieving world, but it also allows us to accomplish far more than we ever could on our own. Collaboration is the key to making a significant kingdom impact." —**James Griffin, Atlanta NewThing Network**

At the same time, we were also planting churches. Eventually, we started enough churches that we formed an organization called NewThing. I will get into more details about this in later chapters when we talk about joining or starting a church planting network.

This organization was helping to multiply new churches the way I had dreamed our church would multiply sites. In a three-year period, NewThing expanded from twenty-six churches to fifty-two to 106 reproducing churches. Most were brand new, and they were all committed to reproducing other new churches.

Meanwhile, Community Christian was still growing and adding a new site every few years. But God was making it obvious that the most direct route to 200 was going to be through starting new churches as a network rather than starting locations as a single church.

To be totally candid, a big part of me didn't want to give up on the dream of 200 locations—even though we only had ten locations and that at this rate, we would get to 200 sometime around the year 2400 A.D! I found it very appealing to do something that others hadn't done before.

I heard Ken Blanchard once say that the three letters in the word "ego" stood for **e**dging **G**od **o**ut. That is exactly what I was doing! My ego had too much of me and was edging God out of building His kingdom. It was then that I realized that not only was God calling me to pursue this vision together with other churches, but He was also asking me to quit pointing to myself and instead, point to Him.

And I realized to do that, a part of me had to die. I needed to repent of a vision that pointed to me rather than Jesus. I had to reorient my life to make sure I was not doing my thing, but rather, God's thing. I had to determine to forego construction on my castle and focus on building God's kingdom. Simply, as a leader, I had to decrease and He had to increase!

Not only was God calling me to pursue this vision together with other churches, but He was also asking me to quit pointing to myself and instead, point to Him.

Movement Starts With God Working Within You

This beginner lesson of every Christian leader that we are better together with God is one that I have had to learn and relearn over and over again. A few years ago, I was in Manchester, England, to speak at the Launch church planting conference. I had finished my talk on what it means to be a hero maker and in between sessions, I took some time to catch up with Ric Thorpe. Ric is the bishop of Islington for the Church of England. Impressive-sounding title, huh? It fits because Ric is an impressive guy and is also in charge of church planting for the Church of England.

I've known Ric for a while; so I was excited to talk with him and hear the latest. I asked him, "How are things going in your part of the world?" He looked at me with a gleam in his eye and said, "Dave, good; it's going really good!" And I'm thinking to myself, *everyone knows the Church of England has been in serious decline for decades! Almost nobody in the UK is a practicing Christian. How could it be "good, really good?"*

So, I asked him what he meant.

"Dave, things are starting to change!" he said, "Young people are coming back to church!" He told me of a recent survey that discovered while only six percent of adults are practicing Christians, now more than twenty percent of teenagers are saying they're committed followers of Jesus. That's three times more of this current generation saying "yes" to Jesus than the previous generation!

Then he added, "And Dave, since I talked to you last, half the diocese in the Church of England now have strategies for starting brand new churches!"

I was shocked, so I asked him, "What's going on? How did this happen?" Ric is similar to me; he loves the strategies and tactics of leadership. But he didn't tell me about leadership strategies and tactics. He just smiled and told me, "It's prayer and fasting."

I'm going to be honest; I wanted more specifics. So, I asked him, "What else did you do? How did this happen?" He smiled again and repeated slowly, "It's prayer and fasting. I don't know how else to explain it except that we just started praying and fasting, and now God is doing something!"

Ric knows me. He knew that I was looking for a silver bullet; something strategic I could do. Then Ric challenged me, "Dave it starts with God working in you. You need to start praying and fasting, and then your people need to start praying and fasting. Then let God work in you and through you."

What Ric was saying to me, in so many words, is what I want to say to you: The Great Collaboration starts with you being together with God. Before God can create a movement *through* you, He must first move *in* you. Before God will create community through you; He must first be in community with you."

BETTER TOGETHER

"Networks are the new space for this exchange to occur in organic rhythm. Networks are important and necessary if we are to witness an organic move of the Spirit at the street level. It's where the local pastor partners with other local pastors around the corner and together they usher in the Kingdom of God as they mutually submit to the greater call of unity in the Spirit rather than submit to the temptation of pursuing individual identity and denominational turfing." - **Michael Carrion, City to City Network**

"Is Jesus Enough?"

I recently heard Brian Bloye, the founding and lead pastor of West Ridge Church and founder of Engage Churches, tell about a conversation he had with church planting veteran Bob Roberts (of Northwood Church and Glocal.net) about fulfilling Jesus' John 17:22-23 vision that we would "be brought to complete unity" (what we're calling the Great Collaboration). Brian shares:

> *Several years ago, I was sitting with a mentor, a friend of mine, Bob Roberts. We started talking about what would have to happen in our hearts, in the hearts of ministry leaders, the hearts of church planters and the hearts of denominational leaders for us to truly begin to collaborate together. We talked about the need for us to be in deep community with Jesus before we could truly embrace the kind of kingdom-minded community with one another.*
>
> *We talked about the need for wholeness. We talked about the need for healthiness in our communion with God and how that could impact the world; how it would impact our own churches;*

the churches that we would plant together and even impact our families. We talked about the obvious need for humility. We talked about the need for holiness. The need to die to self. We talked about the need to have a heart that truly hungers for God.

And then out of nowhere, in a way that only Bob Roberts can do, he posed a question to me that I believe gets really down to the core of our personal holiness and healthiness with God. Here's the question that Bob asked me. He said, "Is Jesus enough?" He then said, "Brian, listen, if you take away all the initiatives, all the big things that we get to do, planting churches all over the world. Take away the church that we actually pastor. Is Jesus enough? Is Jesus enough?"[4]

Ask yourself that question: Is Jesus enough? When you can answer, "Yes, Jesus is enough," you're ready to lead as a whole and healthy leader. Only a whole and healthy leader who lives in communion with God can lead themselves, their family, their team and their church into greater experiences of being together with God—and one another. That's where we're headed next; so turn the page.

CHAPTER 4

Together as a Family

BIG IDEA: The Great Collaboration is modeled
in an intimate marriage and healthy family.

What if she had grown up in my family?

I was sitting in a funeral home, not as a pastor, but as a friend of a young lady named Talia who died far too young. As I looked around at the family and friends gathered for her funeral, I saw a tremendous collection of brokenness and pain. Divorce. Abuse. Alcoholism. Suicide. Infidelity. Talia seemed to never have a chance.

I first met Talia when she was waiting tables at a restaurant where I and a few friends ate breakfast every Wednesday morning. Talia had a great smile (really more of a smirk like she had just gotten away with something) and always a quick-witted comeback. She had a lifetime ahead of her.

Many Wednesdays, I would stick around a few extra minutes to talk to her and over time got to hear her story. Talia's father died in a train accident when she was just six months old. Her family told the story two different ways: in one version, it was an accident; in the other, he walked in front of the train on purpose. Either way, it was sad. Talia grew up without a father, leaving a huge hole in her life.

The void was obvious. The big landscape photo on her Facebook page was of Talia and her son kneeling beside her father's gravestone. In her search for affection and love, she only found abuse from one man after another. Over the next fifteen years, she would bounce from one guy to the next. The only good thing she got from these relationships was a son.

When the hurt and pain were too much, she tried to make it all go away with alcohol. It didn't go away. So she drank more. The pain still didn't go away. After a week in the hospital from almost drinking herself to death, she sent me a text and asked if we could get together.

We met at Starbucks. I'll never forget her first question: "Dave, can you help me believe in God?" I nodded my head "yes," and we started meeting for a white mocha frappuccino every week where we talked about life, living one day at a time and God. I saw her come to believe. It was beautiful. But Talia's hurt never went away … and neither did the drinking.

I was working on this chapter when I got a voicemail from Talia's mom: "Dave, they have taken Talia to the hospital, and I'm not sure she's going to make it. Call me as soon as you can." Talia didn't make it. At the young age of 36, she had a seizure in the middle of the night and died in bed.

Five days after getting the call from Talia's mom, I was at the funeral with other friends and family. Having spent so much time with Talia, I knew her family, immediate and extended. I got to know her friends, current and old, and some of their friends. I liked them all, but as I thought about each of their stories, they were like an ocean of people who were all drowning in their own hurt—pulling each other under while trying to grasp for life. I couldn't help thinking to myself, *what if she had grown up in my family? How would her life have been different?*

My family. I'm almost embarrassed at how good God has been to me. My parents love God and have faithfully loved each other for almost sixty years. They were church planters and have served in churches that loved them and our family for six decades. My siblings love God, and we love each other. My wife Sue is loyal and loving to God, me, and our three amazing kids, Amy, Josh and Caleb. They all three love God, love each other and have been the greatest joy of my life. It feels somewhat embarrassing and unfair when I think about people like Talia. What do you think? If Talia had grown up in my family, how would her life have been different?

I think it would have been totally different. That's what makes this chapter so important.

Love God, Love Others

God knows we are better together. Jesus knew we are better together. When Jesus was asked to prioritize and summarize all the commands of the prophets, he said: *Love the Lord your God with all your heart, and with all your soul, and with all your mind. The second [commandment] is this: 'Love your neighbor as yourself.' There is no commandment greater than these* (Mark. 12:31-33).

The first command to "love God" is the vertical dimension of togetherness. We covered this in the last chapter. The second command to "love others" (more often translated "love your neighbor") is the horizontal dimension of togetherness. This is what we're unpacking in this chapter.

This love of others is meant to include family, friends and others that God brings into our world. For our conversation, we won't spend time talking about the "others" who fall into the categories of the "least, the lost and the lonely"—but they're included. And we won't spend time talking about the community of togetherness known as church and the people we call friends. I fully acknowledge that God's vision for community is much, much broader than the traditional nuclear family. I also fully acknowledge that to be single is not incomplete. There are also a variety of forms of family (single-parent family, blended family, etc.) that God brings together. I hope this book inspires conversations about being together specific to those relationships; it is needed.

However, to start this conversation, I want us to focus on family and go into more depth on what it means to be together as a nuclear family.

BETTER TOGETHER

"Really good people come from really good relationships. This is why Compassion loves working with church planting networks. Good relationships start with the leadership and they spill over to the regional networks, pastors, staff, congregations, church plants and then to the impoverished kids that get sponsored. We find that church planting networks are full of really good people." —**Eric Brown, Compassion International/USA**

Family Is Mission Critical

You know I'm all about multiplying churches, multiplying leaders and movement making, right? Those things are so, so important, but even more important than any of those things are the big ideas of the last chapter and this chapter. You and me living in a community of togetherness with God and in a community of togetherness with our families are the key leverage points for changing the world and accomplishing the Jesus mission!

In their book, *Together*, my friends Geoff and Sherry Surratt explain the priority of family this way: "Your ministry is better when your family is best!"[5]

Please listen to me—if we get family right, the whole world works right! The best way to have exponential and generational impact for Jesus is through the legacy of a whole family. If we get this right in our homes, we give the following generations the best opportunity to experience and share the love of Jesus. But if we don't get family right, everything else is a failed strategy. Simply put, family is mission critical!

God meant for us to do life and lead our church in a way that's best for our family. Your family is the first expression of your local church.

Four Factors of a Family That Has It Together

So how do you do it? How do you live in a community of togetherness with your family? How do you look back after twenty-five or fifty years of ministry, marriage and family and say, "I did my best to lead my family and my church the way God meant for me to do it!" That's what I want. I'm sure you do, too.

It starts by knowing that when you get to Heaven, you will never hear God say: "Great job planting and growing that church. You did it at the expense of your family, but your church made an impact. Well done!" Let me be clear. I'm not one to predict what God will or won't do or say, but I can tell you with full confidence that God will *never* say that.

It won't happen.

God meant for us to do life and lead our church in a way that's best for our family. Your family is the first expression of your local church. If you love and care for them first, then others will follow your example. They, too, will love and care for their family first.

Let me give you some clear next steps. Even better, I'm going to give you some of the best content that comes from my wife Sue. We teach a workshop together called "How to Have a Close-Knit Family That Lasts"; much of the following comes from that workshop where she did the vast majority of the homework. I've added some of my own thoughts to her insights.

The title of this section is a bit misleading. I'm not trying to describe a family that has it *all* together. None of our families have it *all* together. Mine included. But after 30 years of ministry experience, being blessed to grow up in a family that loves God, and having a wife who is an expert on this stuff, I can look at the "together families" I've seen and draw out four factors: God, Marriage, Identity and Time. Let's look at each one and how these four factors work together.

1. GOD: *Families are built on a spiritual foundation.*

A Fuller Youth Institute study of relational dynamics analyzed the warmth of families. The study looked at more than 300 families over a span of 35 years. The findings revealed that the No. 1 value correlated to creating a family of warmth and togetherness is faith. Researchers wrote: *Families in which children and parents felt close were more likely to be families in which children adopted the faith of their parents.*[6]

As I mentioned above, I'm giving you three more factors (and they are helpful!), but decades of experience have shown me that building and standing together on a strong spiritual foundation is the most important. To that end, Sue and I did our best to create a family culture that valued faith in God and faith in one another.

Valuing faith in God

Valuing faith in God meant that we expected our kids to attend church, be in a small group and find a place to serve (once they were middle-school age). I know it's a struggle for many parents. But we figured school attendance is not an option; so why should church attendance be any different?

If you have kids in sports, which we did, I want you to think about this seriously. When you let your kids choose sports over church activities, it speaks volumes and sets a precedent for how they'll make decisions when they get into college and beyond. In his book, *Boundaries With Teens*, family expert John Townsend tells parents to require church attendance. Sue and I have followed that advice without regret.[7]

Valuing faith in one another

Valuing faith in one another meant that doubt was normative, and everyone has their own journey with God. My daughter Amy went through seasons where she struggled in a very real way with the presence and love of God. She later confided that some of this came from wounds inflicted by ridiculous expectations of church people and even some staff. She told me about one conversation in middle school with a student ministry staff where she expressed doubts about God. The staff person told Amy he couldn't talk to her about that unless she first talked to her parents. Not only was that staff member unhelpful, but shaming. That was one of several less than graceful conversations that sent the message to her "you are not allowed to doubt." Amy quit attending church for a season in college; resented church people and because of that wasn't sure she could trust God.

I distinctly remember a conversation we had that was very important to both of us. Amy asked me why I wasn't freaking out about her doubts regarding God and faith. I told her, "Amy, I have faith in you, and I have faith in God. If God is real and your search is genuine, I believe you will find what's real and genuine." Had I lectured, made ultimatums or shamed her, the doors of communication would have likely been slammed shut, and I believe Amy would have put more energy into defending herself than pursuing what's real and genuine.

I asked Amy for her approval to retell this story. As we reminisced, she told me, "Dad, everyone loves the prodigal son story, but no one wants it to be his or her kid. There are no guarantees, but the best you can do is to have faith in God and have faith in your kids." I love that girl!

Before we move on and in the spirit of keeping it real, let me confess three things I wish I had done differently with our family:

1) I wish I would have talked about Jesus more and the church less.

In retrospect, I loved starting and leading a local church so much that I think sometimes I talked more about Community Christian Church and NewThing than I did Jesus. Jesus is at the center of it all—but I should have made the implicit more explicit.

2) I wish I would have encouraged serving more and leadership less.

I love leadership, and everyone in my family has leadership gifts. In my effort to encourage and equip them, I focused too much on "how they could influence others" and not enough on "how they could serve others." Both are good, but I think I tipped the scale toward leadership too much.

3) I wish my family would have seen me reading the Bible more.

Bible reading and journaling have been a regular part of my daily routine for years, but I wish my family had seen me doing it. I remember seeing my dad sitting in the family room chair (and my grandfather too, now that I think of it) reading the Bible. It made an impression. When my kids were growing up, I was usually off too early in the morning and went to a local coffee shop or breakfast restaurant to read and study. And they never saw it.

If you have any questions about what I wish I had done differently, shoot me an email to daveferguson@communitychristian.org. I'd be glad to help you do better and talk about it with you.

Get this first factor right, and the next three will follow.

2. MARRIAGE: *We love being together as a couple.*

"The most important thing a father can do for his children is to love their mother."

I don't know who said that first, but it is absolutely true! And it must also be true that the most important thing a mother can do for her kids is to love their father. I could give you a list of things to help you love being together: regular date nights; knowing your spouse's love language; and getting counseling when you need it. Those are all really helpful, but my guess is you know that the single greatest challenge to loving one another and loving being together is conflict!

Dr. John Gottman, who has done more research on marriages than anyone, says there is one distinguishing factor that keeps marriages together above all others. Gottman says that he can observe a couple *talk* for just fifteen minutes and predict with ninety percent accuracy whether they will need a divorce attorney by simply looking for this one factor. So what is it that keeps a husband and wife saying, "we love to be together"? Not compatibility. Not great communication skills. It's not even both of you being emotionally healthy. None of that! It's all about conflict and how you resolve it. Being able to resolve conflict is the major reason a husband and wife will still love to be together!

That reminds me of this one couple who had been married for over forty years. You could just tell they loved being together. So I asked them, "What's your secret? How do you keep your relationship so strong?" And he told me, "Well, twice a week we go out for a romantic candlelight dinner, dancing, and a long leisurely walk home." I said, "Wow, twice a week?" And he said, "Yep! She goes on Tuesdays, and I go out on Saturdays." Ok, that didn't really happen (sometimes a pastor just has to lighten up a heavy discussion, especially when it's about marriage).

Back to conflict resolution and keeping our marriages together ... Notice it's not the *absence* of conflict, but how to resolve conflict. If you're married, you know full well that conflict is inevitable. You didn't marry a carbon copy of yourself. You married someone with a different personality who comes from a different family and has struggles that are different from yours. Pastor Rick Warren says, "Marriage doesn't solve your problems. Marriage does not create your problems. Marriage reveals problems."

You determine in your marriage you will never say or do anything intentionally hurtful—and that if/ when you do, you will make amends.

And as these problems are revealed, conflict is inevitable.

Research has shown that four topics lead to seventy percent of our conflicts in marriage: in-laws, in-laws, in-laws and in-laws! I'm kidding. But actually, one of the four is in-laws. The others are money, sex and children.

Ephesians 4:26 instructs us how to resolve those conflicts: *In your anger, do not sin.* Sin is anything we do that puts relational distance between us and another person; and in this case, our spouse. So, what does this verse mean for marriage? Is it about always being calm and constantly talking sweet to each other? Absolutely not.

> *Husbands,* it means making sure that you never let a conflict leave your wife feeling uncertain that she's cherished or doubting that she's loved by you! Not in anything you do or say. That's sin.

> *Wives,* this means no matter how mad you get, you never let him doubt that you admire him and that he has your respect. That would be sin.

I like what my friends Larry and Deb Walkemeyer say in their book, *Flourish.* They write that when you demonstrate honor to your spouse, you help them blossom into who God created them to be.

"Honor is how you esteem your spouse. It is the internal price you carry around in your head and heart about the worth of the person you married. In short, it's the value you place on them. Honor is seeing your spouse through God's eyes and then treating them with the kindness and respect that convinces them of their true worth."[8]

Conflict is going to happen. You will get angry. But you determine in your marriage you will never say or do anything intentionally hurtful—and that if/when you do, you will make amends.

We all know couples who seem unable to stop themselves from saying or doing hurtful things to each other. You can literally see them destroying their marriage and family. Truth is, you can have a marriage where you love being together by resolving to make this one very powerful commitment: *In my anger, I will not give in to the urge to hurt my spouse or win the argument by saying or doing hurtful things … ever!* Keep that commitment, and you will love being together!

3. IDENTITY: *They know who they are together.*

Building on a strong spiritual foundation and a marriage of love, the third factor of families that have it together is a clear sense of identity. This is so, so important. Long before your kids come to fully understand their identity in Christ, they will understand their identity as it relates to their family. If you don't give them an identity the world will! Let that sink in. So, take leadership of your family and make sure you give your family a unique but godly identity.

You've heard people make statements about families like, "The Andersons are so cranky," or "The Chans are the nicest people," or "The Garcias are so generous." These are statements of identity. But your family doesn't have to passively wait for the world to say who they are; you can be proactive about creating the identity of your family.

Creating a family identity is proactively determining what others will say and think about your family. This starts with how you and your family talk about who you are and how you behave. When our kids were very little, Sue and I tried to help them understand our identity as a family.

We would repeatedly tell our kids, "Fergusons do _____" or "Fergusons do not _____." And we would fill in those blanks by saying such things as, "Fergusons do tell the truth" or "Fergusons do share" and "Fergusons are not quitters" or "Fergusons are not whiners" (one of my favorites). With each of those statements, we'd help build an identity for our family so they would know who we are both individually and together.

Long before your kids come to fully understand their identity in Christ, they will understand their identity as it relates to their family. If you don't give them an identity the world will!

When our three kids got to the age they could understand the concept of values, we brought everyone together and created a written statement of our Ferguson family vision and values. We got guidance from Franklin Covey in how to do it; but simply put, here's how I think of our vision and values:

Vision - describes <u>why</u> God put us together.

Values – describes <u>who</u> God wants us to be.

We placed the Ferguson family vision and values on the fridge as a reminder and tried to fulfill that vision and live out those values. This vision and values help shape the collective identity of the Ferguson family and to this day, I think each of us would say, "I'm proud to be a Ferguson."

When our kids got to the age that they started thinking about college and careers, we were clear with them: "You don't have to work for a church to serve God. He's got an Ephesians 2:10 'good work He prepared for you to do' and we want you to do that." We were careful to not confuse our calling into ministry with our family identity.

I talked about Sherry Surratt earlier. Sherry is the former CEO of MOPS and one of my favorite voices on family. She was speaking at the Exponential conference on this topic and said, "Ministry makes a great calling, but a lousy identity."

If you let the work of ministry become the primary identity for your family, then your primary identity becomes being a pastor and your children's primary identity becomes being pastor's kids. It's great to love your calling, but I'm with Sherry—it makes a lousy identity.

Build on a solid spiritual foundation. Love your spouse. Create a clear family identity. Now comes the really fun one...

4. TIME: *They do life together.*

Together families ... (wait for it) ... spend time together! And they like it! They are intentional about spending time together, and they look forward to spending time together. It's just what they do.

When Sue and I coach other parents in how to find a rhythm to spending time together, we encourage them to connect daily, play weekly and abandon annually. Let me explain some of what we did, and you figure out how it could work for your family.

Connect Daily

Our daily connecting usually happened around the dinner table. At least five or six nights a week, we sat down and had dinner together. Lots of laughter accompanied good food around the table. Often, we would do "highs and lows" and let everyone share what went well and what was less fun in their day.

Now I know you're thinking, *with all the practices and activities every night, how were all of you able to eat together so often?* One of the advantages of being a church planter is that you get to set the culture and meeting rhythms in your new church. When we planted Community Christian Church, we made sure that we didn't have any regular meetings in the evening. I would cheat and start my day very early and even scheduled elders meetings from 7 a.m. to 9 a.m. on Saturdays to avoid competing with the family schedule. I have no regrets on that decision!

There are so many good reasons to organize your schedule around this daily connect. Research substantiates that children and teens who eat with their families are less likely to drink, smoke, do drugs, get pregnant, suffer from depression and develop eating disorders. There are also studies indicating that children who eat dinner with their family have larger vocabularies, better manners, higher self-esteem, and more resilience. Some of the most interesting research came from the University of Michigan that found the amount of mealtime a child shares with their family at home was the single strongest predictor of high academic achievement scores.

Wow! Not only will dinners draw you closer together, there are a ton of other benefits for your kids as well! And if for some reason, dinner doesn't work for your family to connect, try to find another time. Breakfast maybe? How about after-dinner snacks once everyone is home from practices and activities? Figure it out, but you need to connect daily as a family.

Play Weekly

Playing weekly has looked different, as the kids have grown up. When they were young, we had a weekly family night, and each week a different family member got to choose the fun. We did lots of game nights and movie nights. We still laugh about 6-year-old Caleb making us all watch the movie *Donkey Kong Country and The Legend of the Crystal Coconuts*. That was the longest one hour and twenty-eight minutes of my life! As the kids got older, we might include their friends in a game night or find a TV series we all like and watch it together for a season.

Another way I got to play weekly with the kids was by coaching the two boys' sports teams. I absolutely loved it! Since my daughter Amy wasn't really into sports as a kid, I needed a different way to connect with her. We began going out to breakfast before school when she was in first grade. The following is a blog post I wrote after Amy and I had our last breakfast of her senior year of high school.

> "Twelve years ago, my daughter Amy graduated from afternoon kindergarten and started first grade, which meant going to school all day. That was when we started going out to breakfast together once a week.
>
> When we first started, we would always go to Einstein Bagels and she would insist on sitting at the high tables. She was so cute! She has always been cute! For a couple years, we frequented Caribou Coffee and we would try to get a seat near the fireplace in the winter or on the comfy couch the rest of the year. The last two years, it has been nothing but Starbucks … partly because we both love it and partly because she works there and gets us a partner discount!
>
> I don't remember a single early morning trip where the conversation was so important that it permanently changed either of our lives. But I do remember lots of talk about school, friends, the future, God, family, favorite music, lacrosse, coffee-snobbery, doubts, church, colleges, dating, the poor, how to make a difference, her "junior high girls," Mexico and Rwanda trips, jobs, money, family, owning your 'stuff,' saving for college, grades, graduating early and more. On second thought, maybe the culmination of all those conversations did change our lives. And maybe that is how love, community and a father-daughter relationship grow—one conversation at a time. I am so grateful for those early-morning conversations and each of those breakfast trips with Amy. It's one of those things I know I will never regret.
>
> This week we left our house a little early and made our last breakfast trip of the school year. As we got into the car, Amy

turned on her favorite country music station (she didn't get that from me). When she turned it up, it was Trace Adkins singing, "You're Gonna Miss This." It's a song about watching your little girl grow up and the chorus goes: *You're gonna miss this/You're gonna want this back/You're gonna wish these days hadn't gone by so fast/These are some good times/So take a good look around/You may not know it now, but you're gonna miss this.* I could feel my throat drying up and my eyes swelling. Yeah, it's a pretty sappy country song, but I was feeling pretty sappy. This was our last breakfast trip–and I am gonna miss this.

Take my word for it—it goes fast. Make time for family. You're going to miss it.

Abandon Annually

Family time for us looked like connecting daily, playing weekly but also abandoning annually. This meant "getting the heck out of Dodge!" At least once a year, we got away from home to relax and play together. When the kids and the church were young and we had no money for a vacation, Sue had a garage sale. She raised enough money to buy a tent and some basic camping equipment. So, we went camping with the kids. It was awesome! It was our first trip to Door County, Wisconsin, and we have been back almost every year since.

All three of our kids are now in their twenties, and we still get to vacation all together every year! We continue to be a "together" family, and I'm so thankful!

Families Are Better Together

When Sue and I got engaged, I loved her and I totally wanted to marry her. But I had no real interest in having a family. Don't get me wrong; I wasn't against having a family. I just hadn't spent much time thinking about having a family. But Sue had thought about it a lot! For her, having a family was a non-negotiable. And once again, she was right! Words cannot express how grateful I am for the family that God has given me. I love my wife and our three kids! And being part of a family that doesn't have it *all* together, but has togetherness is both the greatest surprise and joy of my life!

Families are better together! I passionately want that for you.

Back to my question about my friend, Talia: "If she had grown up in my family, I wonder how different her life might have been?" I think I know the answer. I'm grateful she is in Heaven now, but her life was far less and far different than what God ever intended. She could have had so much more and have been so much more.

Families are better together—it's mission critical.

God wants whole and healthy families, but the Great Collaboration doesn't begin and end at the front door of our home. It extends to the people that God has intentionally brought into your life. You know who that is for you? Let's move on to the next page and find out.

CHAPTER 5

Together as a Team

BIG IDEA: The Great Collaboration is made of teams of people with unique gifts and callings.

We weren't meant to free solo.

I just watched the *Free Solo* documentary about professional rock climber Alex Honnold and his attempts to conquer the first completely free solo climb of famed El Capitan's almost 3,000-foot vertical rock face at Yosemite National Park. With no carabiners, no ropes and no harness, he climbed straight up El Capitan with no tools. For three hours and fifty-six minutes, he strategically placed hands and feet, one after another, until he reached the summit. Just one mistake or slip, and he would have fallen to his death.

The documentary is breathtaking. It's also freaky scary. The most fascinating part of *Free Solo* comes when doctors do an MRI of Alex Honnold's brain. They explain a strange discovery: Honnold doesn't experience fear like the rest of us. His brain literally doesn't work quite right. Basically, it feels no fear; thus allowing him to do things the rest of us would never attempt to do.

I think many church planters and church leaders are like Alex Honnold—we dare to do things all on our own that we should be afraid of. We often attempt to go it alone and take solo risks where only one misstep or slip-up could result in a fatal fall. I'm tired of seeing church planters and pastors fall. There's a better way.

I'm excited about this chapter because takeaways are so important. I believe this discussion will help us better accomplish the mission of Jesus—but it will also help save us from ourselves! Because those of us who have enough courage to start or lead a church usually have enough ego to also destroy ourselves in the process by trying to go it alone. I'm begging you not to do it! Don't free solo.

Many church planters and church leaders are like Alex Honnold—we dare to do things all on our own that we should be afraid of.

Made to Work Together

In chapter 1, we saw that from the beginning of time, the God of the universe has existed as a team. In the very first chapter of the Bible, Genesis describes God at work—His Word and His Spirit (Gen. 1:2-3; see also John 1:1-3 and 1 Corinthians 8:6). This model of the Great Collaboration at work brought Dr. Robert Crosby in his book, *The Teaming Church,* to conclude, "The foremost metaphor or model for teams in the Bible is the Trinity."[9]

It's not only God working as a team. He also calls His Church to function collaboratively. The Body of Christ is one of the most dominant metaphors the writers of the Gospels and the apostle Paul use to describe the church in the New Testament. Paul instructs us: "Now you are the body of Christ and individually members of it" (1 Cor. 12:27). He also explains, "To each is given the manifestation of the Spirit for the common good" (1 Cor. 12:3–7) as he challenges the church of Corinth to better accomplish the mission of Jesus.

In Scripture, one consistent pattern across all the leadership roles and references is the use of the plural form: not one apostle, but a team of apostles; not one deacon or elder, but elders and deacons. They are always referred to in the plural. I believe that if Paul were alive and wanted to express this same vision for the Church today, he would use the word "team."

I'm stating the obvious, but you are not Alex Honnold. I am not Alex Honnold. As church leaders, we were not meant to free solo. It might be breathtaking to watch, but the risk is too great and the mortality rate too high. I don't want to fall. I don't want you to fall. We were meant to work together as a team!

Three Commitments of Great Teams

Over the last three decades, I've been a part of some incredible teams that have done amazing work. Several of those teams at Community Christian Church have consistently grown and expanded almost every year since we started. The teams that have come from NewThing have been diverse and multicultural—some of the richest team experiences I've had. I've also been on teams with some amazing people through Exponential. The Exponential team is decentralized; we do most of our work together using technology. It's crazy how much we can do together even though we're not "together."

> The best of teams are made of leaders who, like Paul, are able to say with integrity, "Follow my example, as I follow the example of Christ."

As I look over my shoulder, I can see three cascading commitments consistent in every great team I've been a part of.

1. Great teams are more committed to God than they are to the cause.

Truly great teams are composed of individuals who are living together with God. While the cause coalesces great teams, the cause cannot be the team's first loyalty. The first loyalty of every team member must be to Christ and to Him alone.

When the primary commitment is to the cause rather than to God, it will result in fatigue, burnout and priorities not aligned with God's will. When the first commitment is to each other rather than to God, it will result in a lack of boundaries. But when each team member makes apprenticeship with Jesus their first commitment, they make wiser choices, live healthier lives and become leaders whose lives are worth reproducing throughout the church or organization. The best of teams are made of leaders who, like Paul, are able to say with integrity, "Follow my example, as I follow the example of Christ." (I Corinthians 1:11)

2. Great teams are more committed to the cause than they are to each other.

Another characteristic of great teams is that they are committed to the cause more than they are each other. It might sound disloyal to put the cause before the team, but the truth is that it's the cause that brings a team together and keeps a team together. When we put other things before the cause, we compromise God's dream for what His Church can be and do. I'm absolutely convinced that uncompromising loyalty to a clear cause is part of what creates a team great. Another way to put it: There is never a great team when the cause is not clear!

In Jon R. Katzenbach and Douglas K. Smith's terrific book, *The Wisdom of Teams*, they make it very clear that "the primary objective of the team must be performance results (carrying out a cause), not becoming a team."[10] Their insight tells us that one of the greatest mistakes a team (and its leader) can make is forgetting that the cause creates the community or team.

Why do so many people remember athletic teams or army platoons as the places where they experienced the most genuine community? Because there was a clear cause that created community. The cause of winning a game or a tournament created a team. The cause of defeating a common enemy created a team. Why is it so hard for athletes to retire? Listen to their stories, and it's not the money they miss as much as the team.

> One of the greatest mistakes a team (and its leader) can make is forgetting that the cause creates the community or team.

The Acts 2 church was also brought together by a clear cause—the cause of Christ brought about *koinonia* or community. That first great leadership team of apostles had a clear cause. And it was a cause they were willing to risk for, even die for.

The best teams are always crystal clear about the cause. Turn that statement around. There is no great team that is *not* clear about the cause. A lot of other stuff may get fuzzy, but the cause is always very clear. At Community Christian Church, we are not big on job descriptions. Most people don't know how much vacation time they've used or not used. I don't know the dollar amount on my paycheck. It was only in the last few years that we forced ourselves to create a staff handbook. There's a lot we don't know—but what we do know is the cause. We are all about "helping people find their way back to God."

My friend, Ed Stetzer, came to visit Community on a Sunday. Afterwards, we went out to lunch. I was surprised and confused by the first thing Ed said to me.

"Thirteen times!" he said.

"Thirteen times, what?" I asked.

"From the moment I pulled into the parking lot, walked into the café, into the auditorium and eventually got back to my car, I heard someone say the phrase, 'helping people find their way back to God' thirteen times!"

I loved that.

"Helping people find their way back to God." That's our mission, our cause. It is the very thing that myself and our leadership team are trading our lives for. And I'm not using hyperbole. We are willing to let our hearts stop beating before we let them stop beating for the cause. The six of us who make up the team that leads Community Christian Church are willing to die for the cause of "helping people find their way back to God."

BETTER TOGETHER

"Partnership in God's mission is not an option. By doing mission in partnership, we keep our hearts humble, we learn from others' experiences, we exchange precious resources, we make friends, we exercise unity and we please our lovely God." —**Ricardo Agreste, Brazil CTPI**

3. Great teams are more committed to each other than they are to themselves.

Great teams are committed to God first, the cause second and third, to each other—all before themselves. This means that every individual team member comes with a clear understanding of who they are because of their commitment to Christ; a clear cause because they are committed to the Jesus mission; and finally a willingness to sacrifice for each other rather than pursue their own self-interest.

When a team has this commitment to each other, it fosters trust and a willingness to have hard conversations. In his book, *The Five Dysfunctions of a Team*, best-selling author Patrick Lencioni says, "Great teams do not hold back with one another. They are unafraid to air their dirty laundry. They admit their mistakes, their weaknesses, and their concerns without fear of reprisal."[11] Great teams can look each other in the eye, tell the truth and make tough calls because they know beyond a shadow of a doubt the commitment of each team member is to God, the cause and to each other.

When a team has this commitment to each other, they become hero makers to one another. They put the interest and success of the team and the other first. Each does everything in their power to see their teammates become the hero in the unfolding story and not focused on making themselves the hero. Each team member looks at the other with the belief that "my fruit grows on other people's trees"—one of the favorite things my friend and *Halftime* author Bob Buford always said.

Another friend and author, Sam Chand, says, "It takes teamwork to make the dream work." These three cascading commitments—to God, cause and each other—make the greatest of teams.

> Great teams can look each other in the eye, tell the
> truth and make tough calls because they know beyond
> a shadow of a doubt the commitment of each team
> member is to God, the cause and to one other.

10 Benefits of Teamwork

Hopefully, I've convinced you not to take on El Capitan on your own. By God's design, we were not meant to free solo. Instead, we commit ourselves to Him, His mission and a team—and in that order. But if you still need convincing, here are ten benefits of doing work as a team. These come from the book *Teams That Thrive* by Ryan T. Hartwig and Warren Bird (I wrote the foreword for it). I think you'll appreciate what they've uncovered. If you are already convinced, just skip to the end of the chapter!

1. Greater productivity

As the Bible emphatically illustrates in 1 Corinthians 12-14, not everyone is gifted the same. When each team member fully operates out of various gifts, talents and strengths toward a common goal, instead of constantly trying to mitigate personal weaknesses, teams are able to outpace the combination of individual contributions.

2. Less stress and pressure on the point leader

Teams take the pressure off the organizational point leader, spreading out the responsibility for organizational leadership to several persons. Solomon expressed the power of collaboration: "Two are better than one, because they have a good reward for their toil. For if they fall, one will lift up his fellow. But woe to him who is alone when he falls and has not another to lift him up!" (Ecc. 4:9-10, KJV).

In addition, teams somewhat level the proverbial playing field so that participants lower in the organization can more freely offer their ideas, knowledge and concerns. The extent of the leveling of the playing field and resulting decrease of the stress load on the point leader depends, however, on the level to which responsibility is shared and power distributed among the team (in other words, how the team deals with the notion of "first among equals"—how much first and how much equal).

3. Greater leadership development

By inviting additional staff into the most crucial conversations about mission, values and strategy, and then inviting the team to make key decisions, team members are spurred to develop their own leadership capacity. In fact, inviting a group of emerging leaders into the church's most significant decision-making tasks is a fantastic way to develop leaders.

4. More creativity and innovation

It's a well-trod myth that bursts of creativity are developed in the private closet. In reality, innovative solutions to pressing problems are more typically developed through collaboration with others. Leadership teams, therefore, enable individuals to build upon one another's ideas to create solutions that go beyond one person's limited vision of possibilities.

5. Better decision making

The issues discussed at the senior level of any organization are often complex, necessitating a breadth of perspectives from which to address the challenges. Well-staffed and well-structured teams potentially have more information (because of the knowledge brought by each member) and should be able to process it better than individuals. And they bring together people with multiple perspectives and insights into how to respond to those issues.

6. More safety and accountability

Because teams provide strength in numbers, increased opportunities for cross-training, and promote mutual accountability, they offer stability to organizations in times of distress or change, as well as provide checks and balances to each member's individual performance. Based on his extensive study of power and status in the early church, social historian and pastor Joseph Hellerman argues, "A community of leaders has the ability to maximize a pastor's strengths, while simultaneously intercepting and derailing potential abuses of spiritual authority before irreparable damage is done." News accounts of pastoral sin and abuse are all too rampant and offer a timely, important reminder of the need for accountability with the responsibilities and privileges of leadership.

Similarly, teams provide a setting where multiple people can lead, teach, preach, strategize, counsel and administer, which prevents too much specialization among team members. Though a reasonable level of specialty is warranted, too much of a good thing can put a church in dangerous territory in the case that only one person can effectively teach, manage the books, run programs, etc. Teams create a setting for collaboration and cross-training. Along those lines, Adam McHugh in his book, *Introverts in the Church*, warns "in a [leadership] team setting, leadership is shared by a community of people, which counters the tendency for pastors to form congregations in their own images."

7. Less loneliness

Leadership doesn't have to be lonely. Teams combat isolationism by placing senior leaders in mutually accountable relationships, sharing the burdens of personnel issues, resource conflicts, and difficult decisions that rise to the top of any organization, and developing camaraderie and trust among co-laborers. One of the primary causes of pastoral burnout and turnover is lack of community. Too many pastors are seen, or see themselves, as a sacred person over the church who can never really become a part of the congregation. Teams combat such isolation, pushing pastors to experience community, which they then can use to model community to the church.

8. Greater joy and satisfaction among team members

Teams offer a space where members can voice their feelings, disagreements, opinions, and ideas, and be social as they work. Both of these practices promote finding greater enjoyment of the task and the joy that comes from being in real relationship. The greatest joys of life are found in community; teams create a space for extraordinary achievement in the midst of connection.

9. Greater trust among the congregation

The benefits of a healthy team extend beyond the team itself. Many staff and congregants who are wary of the pitfalls of one-person leadership find great comfort in knowing that several godly people are involved in shaping the direction of the church, determining what to do in difficult personnel situations, and, in some cases, developing what is taught to the church. For instance, though several staff members at one church we visited were sometimes confused and even distraught by decisions that had been made by the executive team, they found great confidence in knowing that one staff member they really trusted (other than the senior pastor) was part of making those decisions.

10. Provide better organizational leadership

Putting it all together, organizations benefit from true teamwork at the top of the organization, as it produces:

- better decisions based on greater perspective and information.
- greater accountability for senior leaders.
- enhanced productivity that reduces bottlenecks at the executive level.
- spread out weight of responsibility among several organizational leaders.
- opportunities for leadership development for more staff members or high-capacity lay leaders.
- greater community and satisfaction among team members.[12]

The best organizations and teams understand these benefits. It's no wonder modern management practice, both inside and outside the church, have embraced team leadership. Let me give you one more story as a reminder of how teams work.

Teamwork Works!

Long before Facebook had 2 billion users, founder Mark Zuckerberg was a freshman in college and afraid of failing a final in his history class. I heard him tell this story. He was in a Roman history class, and the teacher explained that for the final, he would show a piece of art from the Augustan period in Rome. The students had to write an essay on the historical significance of that piece of art.

For Zuckerberg, math was easy, but history was a real challenge. This was the same semester he and his roommate were coding the very first version of Facebook, and he was developing his own ideas about the power of collaboration, community and social connection. The final was fast approaching, and he realized that he had spent too much time on his pet project and wouldn't be ready for the final.

Just two days before the big test, Zuckerberg came up with an idea that could help him and his classmates pass it. He explained it like this: "So, I built this program everyone in our history class could use. The program would show a random piece of Roman art, and they could type in a response explaining what they thought was the historical significance of that piece of art. After they entered their response, the program would show all of us the answers from other students in the class."

Zuckerberg explained, "It was a study tool—but it was a study tool that kind of crowd- sourced exactly what people in the class needed to know for each piece of art so we could prepare for the final using our collective understanding." His class was becoming a team, and he was leveraging the power of collaboration.

Using this precursor to Facebook, they all worked together and studied together as a team. The result? Zuckerberg passed his final and his freshman history class. The professor later told him, "I don't know what you all did, but the grades on that final were higher than ever before!"

When it comes to teamwork, we are better together!

You were not meant to free solo as a leader. Even Jesus did not fee solo. Instead he modeled for us how to live in community and left behind his eternal community, the church as a way to make sure all of us can live in togetherness. Let's move on to the next chapter and discover what the church is and why we need to be a part of it and not just lead it.

CHAPTER 6

Together as a Church

BIG IDEA: The Great Collaboration is experienced
through God's eternal community, the church.

"Church."

Nobody could tell a better story than Dr. Fred Craddock. Craddock was recognized as the "Father of Inductive Preaching." One of my all-time favorite stories that he would tell was about a special community that had a very special tradition: whenever someone new would come into this community, they would have a "carry-in" meal for them in their honor. All the people in this community would carry in something to eat to welcome this new person into their life. Now that was good, but that wasn't the meaningful tradition that made this community so special. The special tradition happened *after* the meal when everyone formed a big circle, including the new person. They would all join hands and start with the person on the right of the new person. If you were in that circle, you might hear:

"Hi, my name is John and I work at the gas station on Main Street. I'm real good with fixing cars so if you ever have any car trouble you call me, ok?"

The next person would say, "Hi, my name is Mia and I love to bake; and people love to eat what I bake, best of all my pastries and pies. If you ever need a baking tip or something for a special occasion, you let me know."

Then you might hear, "Hi, my name is Alex, I do law here in town. I hope you don't ever need my services; but if you do, now you know my name and my office is right next door to the gas station."

And on around the circle they would go. It was that special tradition that made this community so special. Then Craddock would dramatically end the story by saying, "And that special community had a special name. You know what they called that circle of friends? They called it *church.*"

What's a Church?

I love that story and how it illustrates the inclusive, serving and loving nature of this growing group of people. But was it really a church? Was Dr. Craddock right? Or was it just a masterfully told story that makes you feel good?

The church is the only community that will go on into eternity. The church was commissioned by Jesus and created by the first apostles. In 1 Corinthians 12, we have both a vision of the church macro & universal and micro & local. The apostle Paul tells us in 1 Corinthians 12:27, *"Now you are the body of Christ, and each one of you is a part of it."* If you are a follower of Jesus, you are a part of the body of Christ. Like it or not, you are a part of this forever community called the church.

My intention in this chapter is to challenge you to do life together with a church. What does that look like? We'll get to that, but first I want you to pause and ask, "What exactly is a church?" Think about your definition and what makes a church a church.

The next several paragraphs are from *The Mobilization Flywheel* by Larry Walkemeyer and Todd Wilson.[13] Slowly read through them as you try to answer the question, "What exactly is a church?"

You can try asking a hundred pastors to define church and you'll get nearly a hundred different answers. Their answers will probably have many similarities, too. Some will go to the original languages. Others will reach for the Church fathers. Still others will explain the pragmatic realities that shape what they call church.

As our American culture shifts, our technologies empower new communication forms, our population grows even denser in urban areas, and innovative forms of church emerge, new questions are being asked about what comprises "church."

Is the house church —with its sharing of life and Word and sacraments but with no identified leader or accountability for participants — truly a church?

Is the highly organized, liturgical church—with its steeple, gilded pulpit, and formal communion but with no true fellowship, no discipleship, or missional expressions — a biblical church?

Is online church—with its online gatherings and chat rooms but no physical gathering—a biblical church?

Is the group that meets Saturday mornings to pray, study Scripture, and pass out food to the homeless but with no baptism, communion, or elders a real church?

Is the group that goes biking on Sunday mornings after sharing a few verses and prayer an adequate expression of a church?

If we gather in a circle, hold hands and share our unique gifts with new people, is that a church?

Is a gathering a church because we choose to call it a "church"? Is there a biblical definition for when the term "church" can be accurately used?

God chose not to put a dictionary definition of "church" in our Bibles. There is no chapter that gives a sacred list of what constitutes a real church. The exact definition is left somewhat open-ended.

While God has not written a *prescription* we must follow, there is a *description* we must recognize and honor lest we invent our own definitions of church.

BETTER TOGETHER

"Networks allow us to do what we couldn't do on our own. They help create a new reality and being part of a network lets us imagine things that weren't previously possible. It's good to be reminded that we can do more together than we can by ourselves. That is nowhere more true than in dreaming and working towards a multiplying movement of churches. Whether you are part of a large resourced church, or brand new church plant, networks give you a seat at the table as you pursue God's mission together." **—Chad Clarkson, Houston Church Planting Network**

Minimal Ecclesiology

Our goal is not to prescribe what a definition of "church" should be or a universal minimum ecclesiology. We simply believe it's critically important to consider how the following elements fit in your ecclesiology. That's why we've developed the following questions to help you decide on a minimum ecclesiology grounded in history and God's Word:

1. Biblical instruction—What does the Bible say about church?
2. Biblical example—What practices are at play in the Bible narrative?
3. Church fathers— What teachings and practices do we see in the early church fathers' writings?
4. Cultural sensitivity—How can we be sensitive to different cultural contexts without compromising core biblical truths, teachings, and intentions?

As you look at these four considerations, your ecclesiology will begin to emerge around baseline doctrines, practices, and governance.

1. Doctrines— What are the essential beliefs of the church?

   For example:

   - The Father is worshipped as creator.
   - Jesus is exalted and confessed as Savior and Lord.
   - The Spirit is honored as present and active.
   - The Scriptures are authoritative for life and doctrine.

2. Functions—What are the essential practices of the church?

   For example:

   - Worship
   - Teaching
   - Prayer
   - Sacraments
   - Fellowship
   - Disciple making
   - Compassion
   - Justice
   - Mission
   - Global missions
   - Body ministry

3. Governance—What are the essential structures, leaders, and accountability practices of the church? What about elders, pastors, deacons, apostles, prophets, evangelists, shepherds, teachers, church councils, moral standards, church discipline and church boards?

With that backdrop in view, ask yourself what the Bible has to say; what church history tells you; and how you create and do church in your cultural context. I encourage you to go back through the last few paragraphs in this chapter and wrestle with the question, "What is a church?" Don't let it paralyze you from starting a church, being a part of a church or leading in the church. God has a history of using people and institutions that don't get it right. But continue to wrestle with the question and in time you'll determine a biblical minimal ecclesiology and come to a definition of "church."

What to Do About Church?

I genuinely want you to think through the "what is a church" important question, but I don't want you to get stuck defining church and never discover what it means to live together as a church. Work it out as a part of a church. Do it in community and do it together with a church.

I know too many church leaders, particularly pastors (in both big churches and small) who are leading a church but are not really a part of the church. They are the upfront presence behind the pulpit or on the stage, but when it comes to actually doing life with people in the pews they are absent. They are not in a small group in the church. They have few friends within the church. These pastors are leading their churches, but are not really a part of their churches.

The isolation, seclusion and loneliness only mimic what is happening all across our Western world. Look at the numbers. Thirty-five percent of Americans report they are "chronically lonely." Only eight percent of Americans report having conversations with their neighbors in the last year. Another report found that twenty-five percent of Americans say they have "zero confidants." Multiple studies have tied loneliness to heart disease, dementia, depression and anxiety. One study found that loneliness is as bad for your health as smoking fifteen cigarettes a day.[14] After numerous studies, researcher George Gallup concluded, "Americans are among the loneliest people in the world."

God is calling us to live in a different way. Both at the beginning of creation and at the beginning of the church, Scripture reminds that we are better together! As church leaders, we need to live in togetherness and lead in togetherness.

I know too many church leaders, particularly pastors
(in both big churches and small) who are leading a
church but are not really a part of the church.

Live Together With Your Church

In a culture that encourages a very individualistic approach to life, the general sense of loneliness is exponentially heightened in the life of a church leader and his family. In his book, *Pastors at Risk*, Dr. Chuck Wickman talks about the impact of isolation and loneliness on the pastor and his family. He explains that pastors often feel a deep sense of isolation from others—an inability to connect in significant relationships that bring balance and health. This is due, at least in part, to the distance between pastor and parishioners that we often let define our role. Add to that the care-giving functions of pastoral ministry, and the pastor can be left depleted and unavailable emotionally.[15]

So, how to do we end up so lonely in a crowded church? Let me give you at least three reasons.

Individualism

The first reason we do not live in togetherness with our churches is individualism. The same thing that made us think we could plant a church often keeps us from being a part of that church. After the French sociologist Tocqueville traveled through America in 1831, he consequently identified "rugged individualism" as the defining American trait. Now almost 200 years later, that "rugged individualism" has contributed to our independence and unmatched entrepreneurship. But it has also created a quiet desperation of loneliness.

Columnist David Brooks writes, "We live in a culture of hyper-individualism. There is always a tension between self and society … Over the past sixty years we have swung too far toward the self. The only way out is to rebalance, to build a culture that steers people toward relationship, community, and commitment—the things we most deeply yearn for, yet undermine with our hyper-individualistic way of life.[16]

And that's the rub! To live in togetherness, you have to give up— not all, but some—of your autonomy. You have to come under the accountability of other people. To live in togetherness with a church, you have to commit, which means you sometimes miss out on other options. You can't just do whatever you want, whenever you want, *and* still live in togetherness.

Idealism

A second reason I think we avoid living together with our churches is idealism. We get into the ministry with a beautiful vision for what the church could be and should be. It is the idealistic view that also causes some of us to shake our heads in despair and keep our distance. The reason that many of us don't relationally commit to our churches is because of wildly unrealistic expectations. We keep expecting to find the picture-perfect small group, and it never comes! So, instead of going deep with anyone we skim the service with everyone. Soon we have been in our churches for three five or even ten years or more and we have successfully grown a church, but never actually been a part of one.

Intimidation

Perhaps the biggest reason so many pastors are not experiencing genuine community in their churches is because of intimidation. We're straight-up scared of intimacy. I don't just mean those of us who are introverts. Introversion and extroversion have nothing to do with how relational somebody is. Some of the most relational people I know are high introverts. And some of the most individualistic, lonely people I know are high extroverts. We're scared to live together with our church, because we realize that if we really commit to a community, our real self will come out. Who we actually are will come out in the open before God and each other. And we're scared of that kind of vulnerability! We know to really experience community and get the most out of it means letting people know our whole selves—the good, the bad and the ugly. Deep down, we think, *If people get to know me I don't think they will really like me; I don't even like me.* We are intimidated!

Here's the truth: If we are serious about living as followers of Jesus, we can't follow Jesus alone. Every Tuesday night, I gather in a home with about a dozen other people who are also trying to follow after Jesus. Often we share a meal. We always study the Bible together. We conclude every evening praying for one another. We have gone through some of life's greatest challenges: the loss of a child; divorce; death of a parent; financial hardships; the struggle of depression and anxiety and more. We have also grown together: we have learned to love; to be generous; to serve; to fight fair and how to hold doubt and faith at the same time. I love these people and they love me. Together we can get each other through anything—in this life and into the next!

You need a group like that too. I don't care what you call it a missional community, small group or Sunday school class. Togetherness is not optional. Relationships are the catalyst for personal transformation! We are better together!

> We're scared to live together with our church, because we realize that if we really commit to a community, our real self will come out.

Lead Together With Your Church

The Tuesday night small group I just described is also one I lead. Often times, I will get pushback from church leaders (particularly large church pastors) on the idea of leading a small group in their church. They will shake their heads and say, "I can't do everything!" or "I train others to do that." I agree that you can't do everything and I believe you should engage in leadership training. However, I encourage church leaders to follow this axiom when determining where to use their leadership gifts in the church: *lead at the smallest level and at the largest level of your leadership capacity.* Read that again and let it sink in.

How do you *lead at the smallest level and the largest level of your leadership capacity?* If you are in a small- or medium-sized church; at the smallest level, you would lead a small group and apprentice a small group leader(s) and at the largest level also lead in training a leadership resident to plant another church. You would let your high-capacity volunteers, elders and staff does everything else in between.

In my case, I am pastoring a larger church and also leading a church planting network. So, to lead at the smallest level means I lead a small group and apprentice a small group leader and for me to lead at the largest level means I'm apprenticing future network leaders to start church planting networks across the country and around the world. The volunteer leaders, coaches, elders and staff do everything else in between.

Following this leadership axiom—*lead at the smallest level and the largest level of your leadership capacity*— helps you do the following:

1. *Modeling* - You lead in creating togetherness in the exact way you are asking others to do it. By leading a small group, you are showing others how to do it and modeling leadership.
2. *Storytelling* – By leading a small group, you will have stories to tell that will reinforce a culture of togetherness.
3. *Impact* – By leading a small group and, for example, helping other leaders start churches, you are showing leaders they need to continually be expanding and growing their influence by reproducing at every level.

Notice, this keeps you from "doing everything" and allows you to focus on training others for the greatest impact.

Together As a Church

Hopefully, you're realizing that togetherness is not an option. It's not just a good idea or something you can take or leave— absolutely not! Living in togetherness is always a part of following Jesus! It wasn't optional for Him. It wasn't optional for the first apostles. It wasn't optional for the first Christians, and it's not optional for us! This community and the unity of this community are absolutely essential for accomplishing the Jesus mission.

Some of my family's best friends in life have come through small groups. They have helped Sue and me get through some of the rough times in our marriage. They have helped us raise our kids. They have taught us how to manage our money. They have given me an example for how to follow Jesus. We are better together!

If you live together with God, your family, your team and your church, you are ready for what's next. Where we will go next in this conversation is what I have wanted to share with you since the very first word in this book. I want us to talk about church planting networks. I'm convinced that this is the missing piece of the Great Collaboration.

CHAPTER 7

The Value of a Network

BIG IDEA: The Great Collaboration accomplishes the
Jesus mission through church planting networks.

Together, we can do it!

Changing the world is more than any one of us can do—*but* it's not
more than all of us can do together. Still, it's going to require action,
effort and initiative on my part and on your part. So for the next
several chapters, I want to prayerfully challenge you to take one of two
actions:

1. Join a network.
2. Or start a network.

If you're living together with God, your family, your team and your
church, the next step for you is to join forces with the people God has
placed around you in a network.

Don't read these next couple chapters as if these words apply to
someone else; or as an inspirational devotion on the heroic tales of
other Christ followers and leaders. These next three chapters are meant
for you. Together, we can do it!

The reason I believe in networks so wholeheartedly is because I have
seen them work both firsthand in NewThing and in networks that

many of my friends lead. For example, I could not be more proud of the work that Greg Surratt and my friends at the ARC (Association of Related Churches) have done over the last few years— they have planted more than 800 churches at the time of this writing. I'm also grateful to Greg Nettle and Tom Jones of Stadia who has created some brilliant resources to help new churches get started— and they are giving them all away for free! I could name dozens of more networks that are multiplying churches, but I'm saving that list for chapter eight. For our purposes in this chapter, let's focus on the impact and value of networks.

What's happening both here in the U.S. and abroad is first and foremost because of God's remarkable favor; and second, because of how He is working through reproducing networks to create an infrastructure for movement.

I've Seen Networks Work!

At NewThing, I'm currently seeing the same kind of impact with my own eyes! What started for me as a bunch of college friends planting a church with a dream of reaching lost people in Chicago is now becoming an exponential movement of reproducing networks and churches all over the world, helping hundreds of thousands of people find their way back to God.

Let me briefly tell you our multiplication story. We reluctantly started our very first church plant only after God made us. I say, "reluctantly" because while I liked the idea of church planting, I did not like the idea of sending and losing one of my best leaders to plant a church. I say, "God made us" because He really did force our hand and make us plant a new church!

I hired our very first youth pastor with the idea that he would not only be the youth pastor for our church but would someday be the youth pastor to my own three kids. I loved this guy (still do); he loved the kids of our church, and he loved my kids. We had great chemistry.

After working together for several years, he looked at me and said, "Dave, I want to do what you did."

"What did I do?" I asked.

"Plant a church; but I want to do it in Colorado," he told me.

My stomach sank. (For those of you who know something about me, you might be thinking, *Hold it, aren't you the president of the Exponential church planting conference and the visionary of NewThing? I thought you were all about church planting?* True! But that's how I felt when he told me, and I'm just keeping it real.)

Back to the story … My stomach sank because I definitely didn't want to lose one of my very best staff, and I certainly didn't want to try and find another youth pastor. So rather than bless this idea or dismiss it, I decided to put him off.

"Why don't you go out to Colorado?" I said. "Check it out and then come back and we can talk about it." I was hoping this church planting idea would evaporate on the trip.

After returning from a quick trip to Colorado, I asked him, "Well, how did it go?" He had what could only be described as a smirk on his face when he said, "It went pretty good!" I wanted to know, "How good?" "Really, really good!" he said as he broke out into a full grin.

This is where God forced my hand and insisted that I bless this church plant. What I'm about to tell you is the first and only time I've heard of something happening like this so quickly and easily. While smiling ear to ear, he told me that he had met with two churches on this trip who had pledged at least $200,000 to help start this new church. I couldn't believe it!

I decided then and there that if God was blessing this new church plant, I had better do the same! A few months later, I stood with him and his wife in front of all our staff and volunteer leaders, told the story and then challenged them, "If God is sending them to Colorado, then I think he is also sending some of you." We had thirty-five people who quit their jobs and sold their homes or transferred schools so they could move 1,000 miles away to help start this new church.

I thought I was losing a youth pastor; but what I couldn't see was that God was using this to give birth to a global movement of new churches. That church plant in Colorado was the beginning of NewThing.

The next year, we sent a team and a dozen people to plant a church in Southern California. Soon after, we helped plant 2|42 Church in Michigan. Then we helped plant a church in Manhattan. Next, it was Boston. Each week, the lead pastors from those churches would connect via teleconference to talk message preparation and strategy and then we'd travel twice a year and meet together. We called it "NewThing" from Isaiah 43:18,19: *Forget the former things; do not dwell on the past. See, I am doing a new thing!* We were just friends on mission with newly found enthusiasm for church planting and this new thing that God was doing through us.

Over the next couple of years, our circle grew larger to about eleven churches. Soon, I realized it was becoming more common for someone to miss one of our weekly calls and not be missed. We were outgrowing our informal structure; so I suggested we form two networks of NewThing and together we called it a movement. We asked each of the networks to meet monthly, create their own goals for church planting and share lessons learned with each other.

As we began to multiply networks, we began to multiply new churches and also churches that were committed to multiplication. Over the next five years, NewThing grew from fifteen churches to fifty-two to 106 to 148 to 258 churches. As I write this, we are now more than 2,500 reproducing churches and 155 networks, working to catalyze movement in forty countries. And we are humbly asking God to use us to see 10,000 churches planted and 10,000 churches committed to multiplication in all 196 countries of the world.

So, when I challenge you to join or start a network, it is because I've seen what God can do through leaders who sincerely believe we are better together!

If you are living together with God, your family, your team and your church, the next step for you is to join forces with the people God has placed around you in a network.

Romans 16 Network?

A great example of a network in the Bible comes at the end of Paul's letter to the Romans in chapter 16. Do me a favor, read the chapter through right now. Go ahead, I'll wait.

Finished? Without getting bogged down into too much detail, what did you notice? Here are a few things that jumped out to me:

First, Paul knows these people and wants them to know he longs for them. They are friends on mission.

Second, this diverse group of people consists of both men and women, slaves and free, Jews and Greeks; they are all included in Paul's greetings.

Lastly, I noticed there are multiple churches. One church meets in a house; another seems to be led by Narcissus.

You know what I think? I think Paul was a network leader, and what we have here is a final greeting to his network in Rome. We don't know exactly what this network did together or how they did it. But it's clear they were a network and that their relationships were deep.

What Does a Church Planting Network Look Like?

So what does a network look like? In the next chapter, I will give you ten different models and over fifty different examples to consider either joining or replicating in your context. But what they all have in common is this: a passionate commitment to multiplying new churches together.

While the phenomenon of rapid church planting is unfamiliar to us in the Western world, we're not without historical examples. Let me tell you about one you're familiar with.

Today there are more than 200,000 Methodist churches in the world and 51 million people who are part of those churches. Chances are there is probably a Methodist church located near you. While the Methodist denomination is in decline today, it once experienced rapid reproduction, especially in its beginnings.

A church planting network is a group of churches with a passionate commitment to multiply new churches together.

Do you know what one of their keys was to exponential growth? They didn't start as a denomination; but as a simple network of churches and church planters. Methodism started with John Wesley who dreamed of a movement of multiplying churches that would accomplish the mission of Jesus. Does that sound familiar? Wesley, who was part of the Anglican Church of his day, began to enroll others in what he called "the method." Together, he and his friends catalyzed a movement. So while multiplying church networks may seem like a new thing in our day, from a historical perspective they have been around for years.

Church history also confirms we are better together.

BETTER TOGETHER

"A network allows you do more together and keeps the mission in front of you. Leaders need a band of brothers and sisters in the trenches with them, working to advance the cause of reaching the world for Jesus." —**Andy Wood, Bay Area NewThing Network**

5 Benefits of Networks

Hopefully by now, you're starting to see the necessity for being in a network or perhaps even starting a church planting network. Before I give you several examples of network models, let's spend a little time letting me sell you on the benefits of networks. While I could list more than a couple dozen, I want to quickly highlight five benefits centered on vision, relationships, investment, results and kingdom.

1 – VISION Benefit: *Networks dream God-sized dreams.*

Every network I've seen come together has always had a bigger dream than any of its individual parts—one hundred percent of the time! Simply put, networks dream God-sized dreams! Why? Church multiplying networks attract leaders who have a common vision (we called it "cause" in chapter 5 about teams) for accomplishing the mission of Jesus through church planting.

When these leaders come together, this synergy creates tremendous enthusiasm. The word "enthusiasm" comes from the Greek word *entheos* meaning "God within." These leaders are experiencing what Matthew 18:20 describes: "For where two or three gather in my name, there am I with them." When leaders come together, God shows up in a more profound way than when they go it alone. In a network, leaders experience the presence of God, and He gives them a God-sized vision of what they could accomplish together.

Every network I've seen come together has always had a bigger dream than any of its individual parts —one hundred percent of the time!

My guess is you haven't heard about Altin Kita and Kejdis Bakvalli in Albania. You should have. Together, they're leading a movement of small church planting networks that are dreaming God-sized dreams. Only 0.6 percent of Albania's population identifies as evangelicals with only 300 churches in the country. Almost no one! You might say there is no vision for church planting in this southeastern European country. You also need to understand that Albania is predominately Muslim and was under Communist rule for decades when the official religion was actually no religion!

It's in that context that Altin and Kejdis both planted churches. Each church saw some growth and reached people far from God, but they both longed to see church planting movements not only in Albania but throughout the Balkans. So these two apostolic leaders came together to form a small church planting network, and two things began to happen:

First, they started to have a God-sized dream for what they could do together. Here is how Altin and Kejdis explained it to me: "It all started very small with only two church planters partnering together and asking each other 'what if' questions: *What if we trust God to see the number of existing churches dramatically multiply by 2020? What if we trust God to see one church per 10,000 people? What if we reached out to other leaders and shared our big dream?* And lots of other similar 'what ifs?'"[17]

Second, they began to see a movement of multiplying churches. Over the next five years, they saw seventy-three new churches started in Albania, three new churches started in MonteNegro, three new churches started in Kosovo and eight new churches started in Macedonia. And their partnership continues to open more doors. They have also visited and shared their "together" vision in Croatia, Slovenia, Serbia, Bosnia, Bulgaria, Israel, the Republic of Georgia and Greece.

Altin Kita and Kejdis Bakvalli are vivid examples of how networks can help us dream God-sized dreams.

BETTER TOGETHER

"The benefits of being in a network focused on the multiplication of disciples, leaders, and churches is just that—more disciples, more leaders and more churches on mission in our city. The 'iron sharpens iron' relationships I have in my network have helped change my personal scoreboard and the wins our church focuses on as well."
—James Grogan, San Diego Church Planting Movement

2 – RELATIONAL Benefit: *Networks produce friends on mission.*

Let me tell you about two church planting friends, Troy McMahon and Dan Southerland (I've mentioned them earlier). Troy and Dan are the best of friends. They both love cigars. They both love motorcycles. They both love church planting. It was the cause of multiplying new churches and God's Spirit that prompted these two leaders to start two, soon to be three, church planting networks in Kansas City. In just five years, these networks have helped bring to life thirty-four new churches in the Kansas City metro area while mentoring many other network leaders across the country!

At the core of these networks is a group of friends on mission together. It started with Troy and Dan, and then they began inviting other pastors into their circle who also believed in their vision to "transform the spiritual landscape of Kansas City by planting new churches." Now the number of friends on mission has grown to more than fifty church leaders that represent thirty-five churches.

This idea of "friends on mission" isn't happening just in Kansas City. I first heard my friend and colleague Joe Wilson use the phrase. Joe has helped catalyze scores and scores of new networks around the world and integral to his work is helping leaders become friends on the mission.

Many people mistakenly believe that if we just bring people together to create community, mission will result. Actually, it's the opposite! If you bring people together around a mission, community will result. Community doesn't create cause; cause creates community. One of the great benefits of a church multiplying network is that you get to be part of a growing group of friends on mission together.

3 – INVESTMENT Benefit: *Networks diversify the risk of church planting.*

Before becoming a church planter and taking the role of global director for NewThing, my co-author Patrick O'Connell worked as a wealth manager for about a decade. In simplified terms. Patrick's job was to help millionaires and billionaires increase the value of their vast wealth through portfolio management. Patrick has taught me a few things about that world, such as that by diversifying your investment, you mitigate your risk. In the finance world, it's called Modern Portfolio Theory (MPT). If you spread your investment across a diverse portfolio, you'll reduce your risk of severe losses.

Anyone who has planted a church knows that church planting is risky business. Many church leaders want to plant new churches, but they tend to be timid and cautious because starting a church often requires a significant investment of finances and people. For a single church to go all in and plant a new church, it can feel like you're day trading—risky!

But when you're a part of a network, you immediately mitigate the risk involved in church planting in two ways:

1. You now have the collective wisdom of a group of people who have experience in church planting and access to other people who know church planting. As a result, you'll be better qualified to know which new churches have the best chance at being successful and what kinds of resources you should allocate.
2. As part of a church multiplying organization, you'll also be part of starting many churches. You'll actually be investing in a whole portfolio of new churches. Since church planting is risky, there may be some churches that never make the impact you hoped (and prayed) for and even have to close. But because you have invested in lots of new churches, you'll have far more that are making a big impact in their neighborhood or city.

BETTER TOGETHER

"It's not biblical or smart to go it alone in church planting. If you are an island, you will go down. A good church planting network will bring the infrastructure that is essential to multiplying churches. It will also provide the equipping, training and care you and your family will need when times get tough. If we are going to see a wave of church planting across North America, it will depend on strong networks that support and produce healthy church plants." —**Kevin Ezell, Send Network**

4 – RESULTS Benefit: *Networks focus on clear outcomes.*

When we're answering to other people, we do things we don't do on our own. Accountability gets results. It's why we talk to a counselor. It's the reason we hire an executive coach and what makes a personal trainer so valuable. They get results from us we wouldn't get on our own.

Church planting networks work the same way. They help us do things we don't do on our own. Networks get results. I've heard the following from church leaders from all over the world, of every denomination and every age: *I'm tired of going to meetings with church leaders where we all like each other and wish something would happen to strategically reach our city. I long to be a part of something that sees results!* If you have said or felt like this at one time or another, you really need to be part of a network!

Let me tell you a story that inspires me every time I share it. Pastor Nuel Manufor left a thriving megachurch in Lagos, Nigeria, to start a new church called Covenant Light with a brand new vision—not only to be a megachurch but also to continually multiply. He had a clear call from God to start a church planting movement. In the first few years, they planted a total of four churches but had to close two down. Manufor was not getting the results he wanted and wasn't sure what was going wrong.

That was when Pastor Nuel met Matt Millar, the Sub-Saharan Africa regional director for NewThing. Matt shared with him how he could multiply small church planting networks. This pastor caught on in no time; he figured out what they were missing, and things started to explode. The initial network started with five churches; and now each of those churches has accepted the challenge to start their own network. These networks began focusing on planting rapidly reproducing churches throughout the city and country. They were not only multiplying churches, they were also multiplying networks! Recently, Covenant Light launched seven brand new churches all on the same day! Now that's results!

5 – KINGDOM Benefit: *Networks are all about God's kingdom.*

I already confessed to you that what I originally wanted was to lead a church that had 200 locations. The vision of 200 Community Christian sites was partially inspired by the Spirit, but it was also encouraged by my ego. The possibility of that castle built by Dave Ferguson had to come crumbling down so that I could focus on building God's kingdom.

Now I'm part of a collective of four church planting networks in Chicago that have a God-sized dream of *more* than 200 new churches in the suburbs and city of Chicago. These diverse networks are multi-denominational, multicultural and multi-socioeconomic. We have leaders that are Reformed and Armenian; we have those who are egalitarian and those who are complementarian; we have Pentecostals and those who aren't! We have megachurches and microchurches. Here is the benefit of networks: they build the kingdom not individual castles; and networks build the kingdom by tearing down the walls that divide!

> Networks build the kingdom, not individual castles; and networks build the kingdom by tearing down the walls that divide!

Don't You Want That?

Before we move on, let me pause and ask you this. Don't you want to be a part of something that...

> ...causes you to dream bigger?
> ...creates a community with a cause?
> ...takes the unnecessary risk out of church planting?
> ...promises you real results in changed lives?
> ...and is all about God's kingdom?

Don't you want that? Come on, I know you do! You wouldn't have read seven chapters into this book if you *didn't* want it! So now it's time for action!

Join a network.

Or start a network.

Why? I'll say it again. Changing the world is more than any one of us can do—*but* it's not more than all of us can do together. Now, let's move on to the next chapter so I can give you multiple examples of networks to join or replicate.

CHAPTER 8

10 Models of Networks

BIG IDEA: The Great Collaboration is expressed
through a variety of church planting networks.

In diversity there is strength and beauty.

By now, I hope you're convinced that we are better together and
networks are a great way to partner with other leaders and churches
to achieve greater impact for the kingdom. I am convinced that more
networks will lead to more churches being planted. That's why I want
to help you get into a network. My goal is that no church tries to
accomplish the mission alone. There is simply too much at stake.

We are better together!

The best way to help you select and join a network is to take you on a
tour of the various network models. Each of these models is unique;
each has strengths and weaknesses. The locus of control is different
in each one; the interdependence is different. The way participants
interact is different. That's the beauty of having all of these available.
But I can say with confidence that all of them have a goal to synergize
efforts of leaders and churches for greater kingdom impact.

All are designed to make us better together!

There are many models of networks. And in the diversity of models, there is both strength and beauty. I have identified ten. As you read about these network models, ask yourself: which one best fits me and the people I'm leading. Then join one!

As you review these ten models, remember that networks are dynamic structures. Not all networks fit into just one of these models. I did the homework with the help of many others and have attempted to classify them based on our collective understanding of their mission and methods as best I could. The point here is that networks are always finding new ways to achieve the mission. While that can make tracking all of this challenging, I am glad it's true.

1) The Collaborative Network

Collaborative networks are comprised of independent churches that have adopted a common mission (church planting or some other mission focus) and are willing to collaborate on various levels to achieve the goal. The churches in the network are autonomous yet interdependent when it comes to achieving more together. Because they align around a common mission, churches in this kind of network can overcome their differences and work together as "friends on mission." Collaborative networks generally decline to take positions on most theological and ecclesiological issues to minimize barriers for potential affiliates interested in joining them. Mission and diversity are highly valued and success stories feature both themes prominently.

Examples of collaborative networks:

- *Ignite Church Network:* Ignite desires to create an intentional church multiplication network that unites churches who are passionate about transforming their community with a new

generation of churches focused on the transforming gospel.
ignitediscipleship.com

- *M4 Europe:* The vision of M4 is to start multiplying church
  planting movements throughout Europe. They work across
  denominational and theological boundaries to see new
  communities of faith that will display the goodness of God to the
  people around them. M4europe.com
- *NewThing*: A catalyst for movements of reproducing churches that
  starts and sustains small collaborative networks, which plant new
  churches. Churches in NewThing align themselves around values,
  relationships, reproducing, residency and resources. NewThing is
  a global movement with networks in thirty countries. newthing.
  org

2) The Regional Network

Regionally based networks organize themselves by geography. Often,
the goal is to reach the region for Christ. These organizations see
the intersection of mission and relationships as critical, encouraging
churches in close geographical proximity within their network to
collaborate to plant churches. Churches in the same area "own" their
geography and often regularly encourage each other through small
gatherings.

Examples of regional networks:

- *BCNY:* Churches are working together to plant new churches in
  New York, New Jersey and southwest Connecticut. plantnow.org
- *Carolina Movement:* The Carolina movement is on a mission
  to plant 100 new churches in both North Carolina and South
  Carolina by 2028. thecarolinamovement.com
- *Christ Together:* Churches are a unified collective with the goal
  of reaching every man, woman and child in the region with the

gospel. Churches own the 'lostness' in their community and network together to do something about it. christtogether.org

- *Christian Evangelistic Missions:* CEM is endeavoring to reach Iowa by planting churches with a heritage and theology based on the Restoration movement. cemchurches.com
- *Restoration House Ministries*: This network is planting churches in New England with the goal of changing the region's spiritual landscape. Rhmnewengland.org

Did you know? Christ Together has organized six regional movements in the United States with the goal of gospel saturation in each region.

3) The Cooperative Network

Cooperative networks exist to bring together churches and leaders to plant more churches. Generally, the network centralizes the recruiting, training, funding and planting of churches to increase success rates and leave less resources to waste. Churches within these networks often affiliate based on shared theological or ecclesiological values. Usually, member churches help fund the network, which funds future churches. Churches in cooperative networks generally remain in relationship with one another and are led by a centralized board or leadership team.

Examples of cooperative networks:

- *Association of Related Churches:* ARC is an association of churches working together to plant churches by providing support, guidance and resources to launch and grow new churches. arcchurches.com
- *Calvary Chapel:* This network is made up of like-minded pastors committed to the advancement of the kingdom and the fulfillment of the Great Commission through church planting. The network provides resources and training to help

family—inspired by Jesus' love and empowered by His Spirit—is passionate to bring the good news about Him to our neighborhoods and world.

- *EFCA:* The EFCA is an association of churches united around the same statement of faith, committed to Jesus, the gospel, and to each other and exists to glorify God by multiplying transformational churches among all people.
- *Church of the Nazarene:* The Church of the Nazarene is a Protestant Christian church in the Wesleyan, Holiness tradition. Organized in 1908, the denomination is now home to about 2.5 million members worshipping in more than 30,000 congregations in 162 world areas.
- *Reformed Church in America:* The Reformed Church in America is a fellowship of congregations called by God and empowered by the Holy Spirit to be the very presence of Jesus Christ in the world. Their shared task is to equip congregations for ministry—a thousand churches in a million ways doing one thing—following Christ in mission, in a lost and broken world so loved by God.
- *Path1:* New Church Starts (Path 1) is a team of leaders drawn from national, regional, and local levels of The United Methodist Church whose mission is to train and equip new church planters who will start new congregations throughout the United States.
- Acts 29: A diverse, global family of church planting churches, Acts 29 is characterized by theological clarity, cultural engagement and missional innovation. Acts 29 is global in reach. Acts29.com

Did You Know? ARC has planted churches in North America, Ireland, South Africa, Australia and the Netherlands.

church planters and pastors more effectively fulfill
ministry. calvarychurchplanting.org

- *Church Multiplication Network (Assemblies of God)*:
is to equip, fund, and network leaders in the church
ultimate goal of multiplying the kingdom of God a
United States. churchmultiplication.net

- *Converge:* Churches work to help people meet, know
Jesus by starting and strengthening churches togethe
through church planting and multiplication, leadersh
and coaching, and global missions. Converge is one c
cooperative networks. converge.org

- *Excel Leadership Network*: Excel is a coaching coopera
specific calling to support and care for the church plar
network. They are convinced that kingdom growth is
on supporting high-caliber leaders. excelnetwork.org

- *Generate Network / MCUSA:* Generate exists for one pu
to equip churches and church planters so they can see tl
vision God gave them come to life. They are aligned aro
the mission, not methods. They cooperate to multiply di
churches and networks to the fourth generation. They ac
this by funding, coaching, training, networking, credent
and resourcing churches and church planters. mcusa.org/ȷ

- *Greenhouse Church Planting Network:* Greenhouse is a rela
cooperation of churches working together to transform liv
communities through disciple making and church plantin;
Greenhouseplantingnetwork.com

- *Wesleyan Church:* The Wesleyan Church's vision is transform
lives, churches and communities through the hope and holi
of Jesus Christ. The Wesleyan Church has a ministry presen
in nearly 100 countries, more than 6,000 congregations glob
and about 1,600 churches in North America.

- *CMA:* The U.S. Alliance is part of a Christ-centered global
movement more than 6 million strong. Their Acts 1:8

4) The Franchise Network

Franchise networks capture and reproduce the strengths of successful churches, usually birthed directly from them. The churches in these networks develop a model of critical distinctives and plant churches that are strongly aligned with those distinctives. Often, churches share a name, distinguished only by their locations; and a central leader will play a high-profile role in expanding the reach of new churches. The network may or may not prioritize church planting.

Examples of franchise networks:

- *The C4 Network:* Based on Ohio, the C4 Church Planting Network is a movement birthed out of C3 Church. C4 came about as a means to help fulfill the vision to multiply disciples, leaders and churches in Columbus, Ohio, and throughout the state. They exist to partner like-minded kingdom leaders and church planters to reach new people in Ohio. thec4network.org
- *Catch the Fire:* Based in Toronto, this charismatic family of churches is led by Duncan and Kate Smith and a team of seasoned leaders who form the World Lead Team. This team is deeply rooted in key Catch the Fire churches around the world and regularly meets together online to bring vision and leadership to the movement as a whole. catchthefire.com
- *Hillsong*: The Hillsong Network provides resources to help churches grow healthy. network.hillsong.com
- New Frontiers: This UK-based movement is a group of apostolic leaders partnering together on global mission, joined by common values and beliefs, shared mission and genuine relationships. They plant churches, train planters, specifically cultivate apostolic leadership (Ephesians 4) and minister to the poor. newfrontierschurch.com

Did You Know? New Frontiers was founded in the United Kingdom by church planter Terry Virgo and today it has around 1,500 churches working with different apostolic leaders in over seventy nations!

5) The Church-Based Network

Church-based networks are built out of the strong church planting efforts of a rapidly reproducing church led by a visionary apostolic leader. The reproducing church's plants relationally affiliate with the leader and may help start additional new churches. These networks differ from franchise networks because the role of the central church's model and leader is not as prominent. Instead, the church-based network focuses on a handful of mission-driven and theological values, leaving the church plant more room for contextualization, yet keeping a clear identity and alignment with the founding church.

Examples of church-based networks:

- Gateway Network (Gateway Church): Gateway comes alongside pastors to ensure health by sharing resources, coaching and training. This network of churches meets regularly for prayer and training. Gatewaynetwork.com
- *Kensington Church Network*: Kensington is a network of related churches that were all planted by Kensington Church in Michigan. Kensingtonchurch.org
- *Real Life Ministries*: An outgrowth of Idaho-based Real Life Church, Real Life Ministries is both a multisite church and disciple multiplying ministry. Reallifeministries.com
- *Summit Network:* The Summit Network is a ministry of Summit Church based in North Carolina and exists to be a tight network dedicated to planting 1,000 churches together. They are a group

of churches working closely together around a common identity and vision. thesummitnetwork.com

- *Thousand Churches Network:* Founded by Cherry Hills Community Church in Colorado, this network has the goal of planting 1,000 churches around the world by 2050. They do not target a geography. Rather, the network identifies leaders with the right fit and chemistry and provides funding, training and coaching. thousandchurches.net

Did You Know? Many church-based networks provide free resources to churches in the network. For example, Cherry Hills funds and trains church planters.

6) The City-Focused Network

City-focused networks are built around the idea of reaching a single city or metro area for Jesus. They are similar to regionally based networks in terms of prioritizing mission and relationships around a specific geographical area, but usually hold theological values more loosely. There is often a high collaborative value in city-focused churches due to the smaller number of potential churches able to join the network's mission.

Examples of city-focused networks:

- *Austin Church Planting Network:* ACPN is a collection of church planters from across the greater Austin area that works together for the social and spiritual renewal of the city and suburbs through helping church planters accomplish Jesus' mission to make disciples. Austinchurchplantingnetwork.com
- *The City Network:* These churches are dedicated to a broad network of mission-minded churches and pastors in the Treasure Valley (Idaho) to join God's kingdom work in planting,

revitalizing and resourcing gospel-centered, reproducing churches. thecitynetwork.org

- *The Cyclical LA:* This growing collective of leaders is an ecumenical community of innovators that share a common culture and set of practices created to thoughtfully start new churches across Los Angeles. Cyclicalla.com

- *Greater Boston Church Planting Collaborative:* GBCPC is a true collaboration of churches from across the greater Boston region, helping each other plant more churches. They encourage church planting and multiplication movements through dialogue, common vision building and mutual learning. egc.org/church-planting

- *Houston Church Planting Network:* HCPN is a network of networks that come together to strengthen church planters to reach every man, woman and child in the Houston Metro area. Hcpn.org

- *San Diego Church Planting Movement.* Churches in the SDCM collaborate to change the spiritual landscape of San Diego County through local churches working together to plant healthy, reproducing churches. They are aligned around relationships, reproducing, resources and church planting residency. sdcpm.org

- *Transforming the Bay with Christ:* The churches in the TCB network are working to catalyze a holistic gospel movement in the Bay Area that results in spiritual and societal transformation. Tbc.city

- *Association of Hill Country Churches:* The Association of Hill Country Churches' vision is that every man, woman, and child in the Greater Austin Area would have the chance to experience the life-changing reality of Jesus Christ because they hear the gospel from the lips of someone in our movement.

Did you know? Houston Church Planting Network has a residency program that is shared by many partner churches in the network, ensuring planters receive great coaching and support.

7) The Rural Network

Rural networks are an important contrast to many networks that tend to be oriented toward cities. Not surprisingly, these networks are dedicated to reaching rural communities while incorporating a number of characteristics seen in other types of networks, such as assessment, training and coaching specifically designed to reach rural communities.

Examples of rural networks:

- *Dirt Roads Network:* Dirt Roads seeks to establish a network of rural, disciple-making, life-giving, transformational church plants throughout the heartland through residency—sharing common values, best practices, and fueling each other's passion for rural church planting. dirtroadsnetwork.com
- *Rural Home Missionary Association.* RHMA seeks to plant new churches in rural America and strengthen existing churches through resourcing, coaching and conferencing. rhma.org
- *Rural Japan Church Planting Network.* This is a great example of a network with a calling to rural locations but unreached people ... in Japan! en.ruraljapanchurch.com

Did you know? Rural Home Missionary Association has specific training called Town and Country Training, designed to help church leaders in rural contexts make greater impact.

8) The Family of Churches Network

Some churches elect to form a family with other churches. Generally, these churches are highly driven by relationships and shared values.

Their values often include a mission orientation to church planting. Like franchise models, families of churches may share names. But this is typically more a product of relationship than model. These networks may hold theological and ecclesiological values loosely but are likely to share many of the same characteristics. Families of churches usually emanate from an original geographical core, but are not constrained by geographical limits.

Examples of the family of churches network:

- *Church Multiplication Associates*: CMA is a network of churches that encourage one another to multiply. The churches are bound together by the commitment to live out the Scriptures in today's world. The network offers extensive training and coaching resources to help churches multiply at all levels. Cmaresources.org
- *Ecclesia Network*: Ecclesia is a network of entrepreneurial, creative churches and leaders who are on a collective mission to revolutionize the church and reach our post-Christian culture. The network endeavors to share resources and ideas with others both locally and globally. ecclesianet.org
- *Hope Family of Churches:* This is a diverse group of churches leading people into a transforming relationship with Jesus and a community of faith. They are dedicated to reaching New York together. hopechurchnyc.org
- *A Jesus Network*: This is a decentralized "family of churches" dedicated to unity and collaboration. These churches collaborate both locally and globally to bring new initiatives (including church planting) to fruition. ajesuschurch.org
- *New Breed Network:* New Breed is dedicated to training church planters in the principles of the first-century church. Newbreednetwork.org

- *Soma Communities:* Soma is a family of churches that make disciples, strengthen one another, and plant churches of missional communities toward gospel saturation. Wearesoma.com
- *mPact Churches:* mPact is a mentoring movement united to plant, assess, coach and train leaders for maximum impact. Their goal is to develop "impact churches".

Did You Know? The Ecclesia Network has developed specific training called Genesis for church planters starting churches in a post-Christian context.

9) Specialty Networks

Specialty networks are missionally driven and organized to reach an underserved segment of society that's often missed by more traditional networks. Generally, these networks are not geographically or theologically based. Each network develops its own set of training and distinctives based on the population they reach.

Examples of specialty networks:

- *Collegiate Collective:* Collegiate is dedicated to reaching college and university students with the gospel—by equipping, resourcing and networking the leaders who are engaged in or are interested in reaching students. Collegiatecollective.com
- *Cowboy Church Planting.* CCP plants in the culturally distinct "cowboy" culture. There are over 200 churches in an American Fellowship of Cowboy Churches centered around this culture. sbtexas.com/church-planting/models-strategies/cowboy-church-planting
- *GlocalNet:* Founded by church planting veteran Bob Roberts, GlocalNet is a family of churches dedicated to engaging every level of society with the gospel. Their model brings church

planting and multi-faith initiatives together to engage cities and nations. glocal.net

- *Mosaix Network:* Mosaix is a relational network of pastors and planters, denominational and network leaders, educators, authors and researchers that exists to establish healthy multiethnic and economically diverse churches for the sake of the gospel throughout North America and beyond. mosaix.info
- *Rize Church Planting:* Rizes dedicated to planting churches in Asian communities throughout the Pacific Rim. rizechurchplanting.com
- *Virginia Deaf Church Planters Network* (SBC): This network has a specific initiative dedicated to helping deaf church planters reach deaf people with the gospel. sbcv.org/deafplanters

Did You Know? The Virginia Deaf Church Planters Network has training to help planters reach deaf communities in their area.

10) Support Networks

Support networks offer training and resources to church planters that fit a set of requirements and values. These networks may operate in a similar fashion as cooperative networks, but are often independently resourced. They tend to be objective-oriented, seeking to plant churches across a broad geographical area. Support networks may specifically identify high priority zones for future planting or may work towards increasing the number of churches planted every year.

Examples of support networks:

- *Aspen Grove Church Planting Network:* The work of this network focuses on serving church planting churches through recruiting, equipping, funding and prayer. agcpn.com
- *City to City:* This network recruits, trains coaches and resources church planters and leaders to start new churches and networks

in their region with a specific focus on cities. Redeemercitytocity.
com

- *Liberty Church Network:* This network is dedicated to
  making 1 million new disciples by 2025 via a network of
  10,000 local churches connected through 500 local centers.
  libertychurchnetwork.com
- *Orchard Group:* The Orchard Group was born in New York
  City with a focus on planting churches in places with significant
  density (population), diversity (ethnic makeup), disparity (wealth
  gap), and difficulty (few churches per capita). orchardgroup.org
- *SEND Network* (NAMB): SEND is the effort of the Southern
  Baptist Convention to reach key cities in North America with the
  gospel through church planting. namb.net
- *Stadia Church Planting:* Stadia's mission is to plant churches that
  intentionally care for children. They offer an array of resources
  to help churches plant more churches, including assessment,
  coaching and project management. stadiachurchplanting.org

Did you know? Stadia plants churches and helps alleviate poverty
through their relationship with Compassion International.

Now, Join a Network!

I don't know about you, but all of this diversity inspires me. As you
can you see, there are a plethora of networks that exist. Their goals and
methods vary. But all of them are dedicated to synergizing kingdom
efforts to achieve greater impact.

Now that you have a better sense of the variety of networks and the
benefits, it's time to take action! Go back through this list of models
and networks and check out their websites. Then contact someone
from several networks to get more information and prayerfully
consider how you can be part of one. I urge you—don't go it alone for
another day!

CHAPTER 9

7 Questions Before Starting a Network

BIG IDEA: The Great Collaboration expands
through starting new church planting networks.

Asking the right questions can change everything.

In writing *Hero Maker: 5 Essential Practices For Leaders To Multiply Leaders*, I shared about the power of asking the right questions and the story of Marty Cooper…

Half a century ago, someone asked a profound question that fundamentally changed how we communicate with each other every day. This person asked a question in an era where every phone was tethered to a wall in our homes by a short, squiggly cord. In some rural communities, people still used a "party line," where everyone would listen for the pattern of rings when the telephone sounded to determine if the call was for them or for the next farm down the road. It was then that Marty Cooper, a young engineer at Motorola, asked a very insightful question: "Why is it that when we want to call and talk to a person, we have to call a place?" That contrary, insightful question led to a new era of communication and the invention of DynaTAC 8000X, which was the very first cell phone.

The Tanner Institute interviewed Marty Cooper and more than 250 other great innovators like him and found that the genesis of almost every brilliant innovation was asking the right questions. The just-right question can be a disruptive agent, cutting through years of complacency to redirect a leader or team's focus toward extraordinary new insights.

Over the last decade, I and other leaders who are part of the Exponential community have thought a lot about what it takes to start and sustain networks in order to create a church planting movement. What follows are the seven essential questions we believe you need to ask and answer to start a network.

BETTER TOGETHER

"We live in a fractured and fragmented world where we are encouraged to pursue our own dreams, realize our own ambitions and pursue our own personal goals. Networks are a unique and vital means of re-orientating us around a gospel dream as we encourage one another in a global ambition for the glory of Christ and run hard together after the extension of God's reign rather than our own." —**Steve Timmis, Acts 29 Network**

Before we jump into the seven questions, let me make a couple coaching comments. First, there are lots of different reasons and motivations for starting networks. My assumption with these questions is that you are interested in starting a church planting network. If my assumption is correct, these questions will be a big help. Second, as you ask and answer the following seven questions, make sure you use chapter 8 as a resource. Review the ten models and decide if the network you're planning to start will be similar to one of those models or a hybrid of more than one.

With that in mind, let's get to the seven questions for starting a network:

1) God Question: *Where is God at work?*

Author Henry Blackaby understood the power of a great question. When he wrote *Experiencing God*, he simply challenged his readers to respond to this question: "Where is God at work? Go join Him in it." This simple question was the theme of this watershed book that sold millions of copies and changed the lives of millions more.

The first question you need to ask before starting a network is the same question Blackaby asked: "Where is God at work?" If you're bringing together a diverse group of leaders and churches to start a church planting network, it needs to be the work of God—and not your own work!

In my own leadership journey, I have found that the best investment of my leadership gift comes when I see God at work, acknowledge it, join Him in it and then report to others what God is doing to see if they want to join me. So, before you say "yes" to starting a church planting network, make sure that God is clearly at work and He's asking you to join Him there.

2) Leadership Question: *"Who are the movement makers?"*

Movement makers are the one constant in every network. I have never seen a network started or sustained without this type of leadership.

My friend, Alan Hirsch, confirms this in his brilliant book, *The Forgotten Ways*. He writes: "I can find no situation where the church has significantly extended the mission of God, let alone when the church achieved rapid metabolic growth, where apostolic leadership cannot be found in some form or another. In fact, the more significant the mission impact, the easier it is to discern this mode of leadership."[18]

These apostolic leaders Alan writes about are what I call movement makers.

The Association of Related Churches (ARC) began when Greg Surratt of Seacoast Church made the decision to financially invest in a few church planters. Turned out that this handful of church planters had a number of leaders in it who had apostolic gifts. This was a group of movement makers! Greg and this group admit to having little experience but a confidence that God was calling them to plant new churches. All Greg asked of these other church planters was that in return they would invest that same amount in other new church plants. And that was the beginning of ARC.

When you hear the words "apostolic leader," who comes to mind? Go ahead and think of a couple leaders. Perhaps the names that come to mind are pastors who write the best-selling books and lead large parachurch organizations or megachurches. If we think about it in terms of contemporary history, names like John Wimber come to mind. It was Wimber who back in the 1980s started the Vineyard Church movement that now has more than 2,400 churches worldwide. Or a little farther back, we think of Aimee Semple McPherson who in the 1930s founded the Foursquare Church, which now has more than 60,000 churches in 144 countries. Apostolic leaders are to the church what LeBron James is to basketball or Tom Brady is to football. These people are the Hall of Famers, right?

Well, while it's true that many of these well-known spiritual leaders likely have the gift of apostolic leadership, I want to suggest that so do some of you reading this book. And so do some of the people around you, such as your friends and colleagues.

When you start a church planting network, the rate of success dramatically increases when you start with two apostolic leaders working together.

When Jesus wanted to catalyze His movement, His first priority was choosing twelve apostolic leaders. These were not "Hall of Famers" but instead a ragtag hodgepodge of a group made up of fisherman, some uneducated, many working-class. They didn't think they had much to offer. I'm saying this to remind you—you do not have to be Tom Brady, but you should have an apostolic gifting to start a network.

Something else Jesus did that we should consider imitating—He sent out His disciples in pairs. I think Jesus knew they would be better together! Being a witness to the birth of dozens and dozens of networks, it has been my observation that when you start a church planting network, the rate of success dramatically increases when you start with at least two apostolic leaders working together.

I'll get very specific about three traits that will help you identify apostolic leadership in both you and others.

Apostolic leaders see the future clearly.

They are able to see a better tomorrow and vision cast in such a way that others want to give their energy and resources to turn that new tomorrow into a reality—today!

Apostolic leaders start new things.

Entrepreneurial by nature, these leaders start something from nothing and empower others to do the same. Wherever life takes them, they leave a legacy of new small groups, missional communities, sites or churches full of Christ followers.

Apostolic leaders embed and guard the truth.

They instill the ideology and values of the gospel into these new communities of Christ followers. When necessary, they also defend the truth of the gospel when it's not upheld.

To help you better understand that apostolic leadership is important but more common than you think, let me go back to my Tom Brady sports analogy. Because the apostolic gift is a lot like being a quarterback on a football team. You need every position to make a complete team but without a solid quarterback, you have no chance of being a winning team. Make no mistake: the quarterback is a special and needed position.

Still, consider that every year there are ninety quarterbacks who play on NFL teams, and every year there are fifteen to thirty more who get drafted. In college football, there are more than 1,500 quarterbacks who play on football teams and a whopping 200,000 that play quarterback in high school every year. My point is this: Yes, the quarterback position is critical, but there are a lot of them out there.

In the same way, we have more apostolic leaders out there than what we believe to be available. It's up to us to identify, encourage and equip them because these apostolic leaders are the movement makers who will lead networks.

So, who are the movement makers? A church planting network must have them!

3) Vision Question: *"What is the dream?"*

Every January on MLK day, I watch Dr. Martin Luther King's famous "I Have a Dream" speech on video, as he inspired hundreds of thousands of people on the steps of the Lincoln Memorial. I love it when he leaves his notes, looks to the sky and begins speaking from his heart saying, "I have a dream … I have a dream that my four little children will one day live in a nation where they will not be judged by the color of their skin but by the content of their character…" The dream of this one man catalyzed an entire movement that united diverse people from different backgrounds. And it is a dream (and speech) that still inspires people decades later.

Something profoundly spiritual occurs when movement makers share their dream for changing a town, a city or a region. That's why big dreams are a critical component to starting a network. The big dream awakens what has been asleep. It focuses the energy of divergent leaders and artists and centers them on a common cause. The big dream of a movement maker motivates us to be on mission and gives us a glimpse of what a new tomorrow will be.

Drew Hyun had a big dream to see new churches planted in the urban context. Specifically, Drew wanted to see God multiply new churches that value multiethnicity, Spirit-filled ministry, emotional health, and mission. As a result of that vision, Hope Church NYC's family of churches was birthed in 2012. As of this writing, they have started nine diverse Hope churches across New York City and surrounding areas. And the vision has expanded beyond that family of churches to give life to the New City Network, which to date has helped start twenty-three other churches in urban areas around the world.

One of the guys who pushed me constantly to dream bigger was Lyle Schaller. Google him if you don't know the name. Over and over, this venerable voice would give me grief by poking me in the chest and then he'd look me in the eye and say, "Dave, your biggest problem is that I have a bigger vision for your church than you do!" And every time he'd say that, it would enlarge my dream.

Something profoundly spiritual occurs when movement makers share their dream for changing a town, a city or region.

Recently, I listened to a podcast with Lifechurch.tv's Craig Groeschel while working out. I almost lost my footing on the treadmill when Craig started talking about an old guy he hired as a consultant. He talked about this guy who would fly into Oklahoma City and "poke me in the chest and then look me in the eye and say, 'Craig, your biggest problem is that I have a bigger vision for your church than you do!'" Right then, I knew that Lyle Schaller had claimed another one of us.

Then I thought, *maybe that is all Lyle did—write books, consult churches and poke pastors in the chest, saying, "Your biggest problem is that I have a bigger vision for your church than you do!"* It worked on me!

I want to be that for you. As you read these words, imagine that I'm poking you in the chest saying, "C'mon, don't let me or anyone else have a bigger vision for how God can use you than you." *Do you have an apostolic gift? Do you meet the definition of a movement maker? It is your big dream that will inspire and motivate others to action.* Start dreaming about what a network could do for your town or city or region. Just imagine!

4) Ideology Question: *"What are the radical minimums?"*

Once you are able to clearly express and articulate the big dream of a network, then you need a simple ideology. Your ideology has the potential to transform casual friendships into a cause-related community of brothers and sisters in Christ.

I'm intentionally choosing to use the term "ideology" because it integrates both theology and philosophy. Ideology includes the important biblical and doctrinal commitments, as well as the unique ways of doing and being. Both are essential elements that hold a network together.

For example, at NewThing, our ideology is built on a theological foundation that Jesus is Lord and agreement on historical statements such as the Lausanne Covenant and the Apostles' Creed. Our philosophy is summed up very simply in the 4 R's:

Relationships: We are friends on mission who commit to meeting together as a network every month to accomplish our vision of multiplying churches.

Reproducing: We commit to working together to reproduce sites, churches and networks—doing together what we could not do on our own.

Resources: We commit to pool together our leadership and financial resources to enable us to accomplish our vision of multiplying churches.

Residency: We commit to developing at least one resident per site/church per year to equip them to reproduce a new site or church.

I refer to this simple ideology as our "radical minimums." You may decide that you want more theological boundaries than that. You may decide that you want to more narrowly define the types of churches you want to plant. Ask the question. Figure it out.

When Stadia asked this question, they came up with the following five values they want all their churches to buy into:

Children: We believe children are close to the heart of God, so they are close to the heart of Stadia. Since the majority of those who make a decision to follow Jesus do so before the age of 18, it is vital that our churches reach the hearts of our children.

Urgency: There are more than 7 billion people on this planet—7 billion people whom God desperately and deeply loves. People who need the hope of Jesus. We must pursue God's people while we are able so that as many as possible may accept and understand the love of Jesus.

Relationships: All great partnerships are built on the foundation of meaningful relationships. Just as Jesus stepped near to build a relationship with us, we must step near others to build trust and foster generous collaboration that can change the world. We believe that together, we are better!

Impact: Stadia partners with high-impact leaders to plant high-impact churches. We discover and prepare planters as well as seek out strategic partnerships that ensure our new churches will change their communities and the world with the hope of Jesus Christ.

Celebration: When there is a party in Heaven, there should be a party here on earth! Life is a gift and Jesus is a gift, so new life in Jesus is the greatest gift of all! Let's celebrate it every chance we get!

Just remember when starting a network, you need to decide what are the radical minimums that everyone must agree upon to be a part of this network. Let me encourage you to process your response to this question in prayer. Then do everything you can to keep it simple.

Simple to understand and simple to say. Simple is reproducible, and church planting networks need to reproduce.

In what has been called a manual for gospel multiplication (*The Spontaneous Expansion of the Church*), early 20th-century author Roland Allen explains why keeping it simple has always been important:

> "... *Thus St. Paul seems to have left his newly founded churches with a simple system of gospel teaching, two sacraments, a tradition of the main facts of the death and resurrection, and the Old Testament. There was apparently no form of service, except of course the form of the sacraments, nor any form of prayer, unless indeed he taught the Lord's Prayer ... This seems to us remarkably little. And yet is it possible that it was precisely the simplicity and brevity of teaching which constituted its strength ... By teaching the simplest elements in the simplest form to the many, and by giving them the means by which they could for themselves gain further knowledge, by leaving them to meditate upon these few fundamental truths, and to teach one another what they could discover, St. Paul entrusted that his converts should really master the most important things.*"[19]

What are your radical minimums? What is your simple ideology? They are important and critical questions you will need to wrestle with before starting a church planting network. Now, let me give you the last three questions you'll need to answer.

Imagine that I'm poking you in the chest saying,
"C'mon, don't let me or anyone else have a bigger
vision for how God can use you than you."

5) Movement Question: *"How will it reproduce?"*

When I first read David Garrison's book, *Church Planting Movements*, it messed me up pretty good. It also confirmed for me that reproduction and scaling are absolutely essential for launching and growing a network. If a church planting network doesn't reproduce, then something's wrong or missing.

Garrison is very specific about what a church planting movement should look like: "First, a church planting movement reproduces rapidly," he writes. "Within a very short time, newly planted churches are already starting new churches that follow the same pattern of rapid reproduction ... Movements always outstrip the population growth rate as they race toward reaching the entire people group."[20]

Garrison's telling us that every church planting network that aspires to see movement should have an infrastructure that's rapidly reproducing.

> If a church planting network doesn't reproduce,
> then something's wrong or missing.

So, how do you ensure the network you're leading will reproduce? Great question! First (and please hear this), you can't guarantee it. God has something to say about the growth of His Church. Second, it should be embedded in your mission statement. The Acts 29 network is not bashful; they declare it boldly in their mission statement: "We are about one thing: church planting. We exist to encourage, resource, facilitate, support and equip churches to plant churches that will plant church-planting churches." That is the stuff of movement!

Third, there are actually a couple things you can control and need to do. I call them the two "must-do's" for every movement maker wanting to see their network reproduce new churches:

#1 Model reproducing.

If you want to lead a network that reproduces, you need to be a reproducing leader. As I said earlier, I lead a small group, and I try to always have at least one apprentice leader. The goal is to develop the apprentice leader(s) to release and take over the group or lead their own group. And I also work to develop church planting network leaders all over the world who are apprenticing other new network leaders. If you move into a network leader role, I encourage you to model it. For you this might mean leading a small group and reproducing small group leaders. But it will also mean that you will always have at least one leadership resident who is in training to plant a new church. As the network scales and grows, you may find yourself reproducing at a different level. No matter what, as a network leader make sure you model it!

#2 Expect reproducing.

In the same way that you model reproduction and expect it of yourself, you should also expect it of other leaders in your network and of your network as a whole. Let me give you a couple tips.

First, ask every leader to make a commitment to reproducing at every level just like you are. Ask them to annually put in writing their reproducing plan. This plan could include reproducing groups, teams, services, sites, leadership residents or new churches. Within NewThing, we use a document we call an MRP ("my reproducing plan"—you can find a sample in the appendix) with all our leaders. When you meet with those leaders in your network, ask them to update you on their plan and how you can assist them in achieving their goals. This is important because if you want to have a reproducing network, it needs to be made up of reproducing leaders.

Second, your network should make an annual commitment to reproducing together. No matter how big or small your network, leaders should come together and make a commitment to collaborate to plant more reproducing churches. This commitment should be documented so everyone has access to it; and it can be reviewed and updated as needed.

Modeling and expecting reproduction may be simple to understand, but they're also hard to repeat consistently. Focusing on these two specifics and repeating them turns the flywheel. In time, this flywheel builds momentum as you model reproduction and expect it month after month. Year after year, the flywheel continues to turn faster. There are no shortcuts. That's how you begin to see healthy rapid reproduction and create movement!

6) Resource Question: *"How will it be financially sustainable?"*

There are three simple components to every network: cause, community and corporation. The cause is the dream and vision of the network. The community is the camaraderie and friendships. And the corporation is the organization behind it. You need all three. Neglect any of these and you will fail. Pastoral leadership tends to excel particularly in community and cause. We often have the least expertise or appetite for corporations. And at the center of organizing a network is the resource question, "How will it be financially sustainable?" There are three basic responses to the resource question that every new network must answer.

"It's free."

The simplest and easiest way to make a network financially sustainable is to have no budget and for it to cost participants nothing. This will require that the network is run by all volunteers. If the intention is to keep the network small and local, then this could be a great way to go. You will spend no money on overhead and all the dollars committed to church planting will go directly to new church plants and not staff, creating websites, and running programs.

While there is much that I like about the simplicity of making the network free, there are some downsides. Without an advance commitment of resources by participants in the network, it is hard to know if you will have the money to plant new churches. Since the commitment level is low it can easily create a low commitment network that accomplishes very little.

The dream of the network should influence your response to the resource question. If your dream is to stay local and be very nimble, free is great! If your dream is to expand across a city and region, free may not get you there.

"You give a percentage."

When asking the resource question, a second possible response is, "We all give a percentage of our total annual budget." The upside to this response is at least twofold: first, it feels equitable and that what is expected of big churches and small churches is the same, but on a percentage basis. The second strength is that if you have a few larger churches, this can be a sizeable amount and will allow you to plant more churches. The downside is that it feels like a tax for expansion and growth and it can create the question, "percentage of exactly what…?" In a church planting network, you want leaders and churches that want to give and not have to give or feel penalized for growing.

"There is a flat fee."

A final response to the resource question is: "Yes, there is a flat fee for anyone in the network of $$." When I realized that I had started a network and was working through these types of questions, I had the advantage of talking to the man I mentioned before, legendary church consultant Lyle Schaller. Lyle lived in the same town as me and would often have me come over to his house where I could pepper him with questions. I distinctly remember discussing the resource question with him. He told me, "You want everyone to have some 'skin in the game' so you don't want to make it free. You should ask for a flat fee from all the churches participating in the network. If you ask for a percentage of their giving, it will penalize churches for growing and it can create an adversarial relationship."

So, when we started NewThing, we asked churches for a flat fee that they would put into their local network for church planting, but would not be spent by a centralized organization. The amount was enough that created a high commitment, but not so much as to keep some out. And when it came time to chip in to plant new churches, many gave much more than the flat fee.

Of all the questions, this will probably be the one you will not want to deal with or think about. Don't neglect the resource question. You can't say, "I don't know." Answering the resource question is critical to the success of starting a network.

7) Relationship Question: *"What are the relational rhythms?"*

Your network needs to be made up of friends. It's that simple and, admittedly, that challenging. The leaders in your network need to learn to trust one another, believe in each other, love like brothers and sisters and even be willing to sacrifice for each other. And it's the network leader's role to nurture and facilitate those kinds of friendships. If you can do that, this network will be an unstoppable force because at that point, you're fostering a cause-created community or what Alan Hirsch (yes, I quote Alan a lot because I love how he thinks deeply about things) calls *communitas*. It's a Latin term that describes a cause-driven community.

You know you have communitas in a network when a group of friends come together for the cause of Christ and leave behind any "this network exists for me" thinking; and instead move together toward, "I exist for the network; and the network exists for others."

BETTER TOGETHER

"Through Christ Together's engagement in eighty-eight networks in cities across North America we have seen first hand what can happen when you bring churches and denominations together for a shared outcome. When this occurs, the kingdom impact is far greater than simply what one church, or one denomination can do by themselves. Not only are these networks planting more churches, but it's a sustainable model for churches committed to the priority of multiplication. There is greater energy, more resources, broader encouragement, and best-practice from the collective genius that God has brought together in that place. It is beautiful to see what can happen when no one cares who gets the credit other than Jesus!"
—Will Plitt, Christ Together

And the best way to create communitas is through what I call "relational rhythms." These relational rhythms are intentional meetings that focus on the cause *and* in the process build community. Again, keep it simple. Here are three relational rhythms I've seen used effectively as a network is starting. As the network grows in numbers and geography, you will need to expand, but these are good starting points.

Monthly one-on-one

A monthly check-in or coaching conversation from the network leader to each church leader in the network. This can be sitting down for a meal together; or as simple as a phone call just to touch base and check in.

Monthly N.E.T.work meeting

This monthly meeting that gathers everyone from the network into one place is a must. You'll want to include three elements:

N – Numbers

Review the church planting and reproducing goals you've set as a network and give an update on the progress you've made. I know for some this is not the most exciting conversation. You'll be tempted to skip over this, but please don't. Make sure you review the numbers every time. Try to illustrate the numbers with stories and examples of new churches started. People, especially church leaders who are used to hearing numbers every week, will need specifics about how their time and energy is being used and working toward.

E – Eat

If you want a meeting to go really well, share a meal! If you want people to like each other and for them to like you, show some hospitality! In some cases, it might mean light snacks. I know of some networks that opt for cigars. I trust you to figure it out; but remember you're creating communitas and you want this group of leaders to become friends on mission together.

T – Training

Offer the leaders in the network some added value training. It should be helpful for leaders but also something they can repurpose and share with their staff or volunteer leaders in their own church. Enlist someone in your network to lead it; or tap an outside organization to come in and provide effective training. This added-value training will bring in new leaders and is one more reason to be a part of this network.

Annual gathering

Every network needs an annual retreat or gathering that spans at least two days and a night. This is a time to give updates on what's been accomplished, renew relationships and cast a vision for the future. Many networks are also part of a larger movement or organization so I encourage you to participate in a gathering with other networks and network leaders once a year. Many use the Exponential conference as their annual gathering ... and I doubt you'll be surprised to hear me say I strongly recommend that. ☺

Albert Einstein had this to say about asking the right questions: "If I had an hour to solve a problem and my life depended on it, I would use the first fifty-five minutes determining the proper question to ask, for once I know the proper question, I could solve the problem in less than five minutes."

There is a lot of time and experience spent narrowing down the questions to those seven. Ask those questions and prayerfully decide if God is calling you to start a network.

Better Together

So, now you have a choice...

Join a network.

Or start a network.

Let's acknowledge what God has been telling all of us since the beginning of time—we are better together! If you're convinced, like me that we are better together, then joining a network or starting one are the only two options. And as I will share with you in the next chapter, it's also the answer to a 2,000-year-old prayer.

CHAPTER 10

We Are the Answer to Jesus' Prayer

BIG IDEA: The Great Collaboration is
the answer to Jesus' prayer.

We began our conversation by learning about the diabolical experiment of King Frederick II and then asking what's killing the body of Christ? In the same way, let's wrap up with a remarkable story of how continually being together saved the life of a child named Daniel and then discuss how we can heal the body of Christ.

Daniel spent the first seven years of his life always sleeping in a sitting-up position. That's how he slept in the Romanian orphanage he lived in with more than one hundred other children. Every night, he was forced to sleep in a crib with another child. It was too small for either child to lie down, so they both were forced to sleep sitting up.

During those seven years, he didn't go to school; he didn't go outside and he only left the crib to eat or go to the bathroom. There were adults present during the day and others who kept watch at night, but he can't recall any of their names or a single interaction.

Meanwhile, in Euclid, Ohio, Heidi Solomon and her husband Rick were going through a home study to adopt a child when she saw a picture of Daniel in a brochure. Heidi can't explain why, but his picture seemed to illuminate.

"I think this is supposed to be our son," she told Rick.

Several weeks later, the Solomons flew to Romania. When they got off the plane, a little dark-haired seven-year-old boy named Daniel stood in front of them dancing and excited to greet them.

The first six months for this new family were filled with lots of "firsts" and lots of joy. Adoption and being parents was going much easier than either Rick or Heidi anticipated.

But then at Daniel's first birthday party with his new family, the honeymoon ended. Since he had never had a birthday, Daniel had never thought about being born or having a family and had never wondered why he was abandoned and left in an orphanage. Now he had all of those questions and that brought on an out-of-control rage that ravaged his adopted parents.

Daniel's tantrums were tornadoes of anger. Over the next year, he pounded hundreds of holes in the wall of his room. He attacked Heidi, leaving her with a black eye and then laughing about it. Another time in the kitchen, he held a knife to his new mother's throat and threatened her. He became so violent they were calling the police several times a month and eventually hired a bodyguard. They bought him a puppy, and he tried to strangle the dog. The next few years were a daily nightmare.

When Daniel was ten, their case manager told Heidi, "Here is what I think is going to happen: Daniel is going to hurt you; you are going to end up in the hospital; he will be in juvenile detention, and your husband is going to leave you."

The case manager explained that Daniel suffered from detachment disorder and was unable to connect to other people. This disorder came from never bonding with a parent as a baby. This meant that he would never feel empathy, would never have a conscience and therefore could hurt other people without feeling guilty. The case manager told her they had done everything they could and should consider other options than Daniel living with them.

But Heidi refused to give up on Daniel. She began to use a radical approach to re-parenting him called "attachment therapy" developed by Dr. Ronald Federici. This new tactic would mean that Heidi would spend every moment together with Daniel. The goal was to recreate the bond of a newborn baby and a mother that Daniel never experienced. This meant they would never be more than three feet apart. So she and Daniel were constantly together for the next several months.

If he was on the couch, she was together with him. If Daniel was in the backyard playing, his mother was together next to him. If he was reading a book, Heidi would cuddle right up next to him. If Daniel didn't comply, the punishment was a hug. Every night, both Heidi and Rick would cradle Daniel between them and hold him while eating ice cream as a bribe. They'd all be as close together as possible for twenty minutes every evening.

Daniel, now in his 20s, says, "After constantly being together, something changed … I started to realize that they really loved me." Heidi, Rick and Daniel will all tell you that it was being together that cured him of his violent behavior—it was gone for good! It was then that he started talking about what had happened in the orphanage. He began to behave appropriately in a classroom. He made friends with other kids. A transformation began to take place. It was intentionally, relentlessly and lovingly being together that saved Daniel's life.

We are better together.

BETTER TOGETHER

"Network collaboration works! it gets us out of our myopic, local church thinking and into hyperoptic kingdom thinking." **—Bob Bouwer, Northwest Indiana NewThing Network**

Is the Church Suffering from Detachment Disorder?

As I think about the Church and where we are today, Daniel's story brings up some compelling questions:

If attachment therapy can save a human life, can being together bring life to the body of Christ?

If being family can heal a person, can living in community heal our churches?

If the church is made of people who thrive when they are together and fail to thrive when on their own, doesn't it make sense that the body of Christ will flourish when we come together; and perish when we abandon one another?

I would respond to all three questions with a loud and emphatic "Yes!"

We are better together.

The Withdrawn Western World

We have to bring the Good News of the Great Collaboration to our churches. Our people are lonely. Our leaders think they have to do it on their own. Our church plants are orphaned. My diagnosis of the Western church tells me that we have a failure to thrive and that we are suffering from a detachment disorder.

Back in the early 1940s, a famous study on the London Blitz bombing raids of World War II was released. The study found that the rates of depression went *down* during the Nazi bombardment, and then after it was all over, it went back to normal levels. Which is kind of bizarre. The interpretation of the data was not that people have an odd love affair with being bombed; rather, they loved the sense of community that resulted in response to the crisis and the way it brought London together. Cities are notorious for loneliness; you're surrounded by tens of thousands of people but often have very few long-term, in-depth relationships. However, there was something about the Blitzkrieg that brought the city of London, and the West as a whole, together.

> My diagnosis of the Western Church tells me
> that we have a failure to thrive and that we are
> suffering from a detachment disorder.

Since then, individualism has been running rampant in the West, and there's been a rapid decline in community. In 2018, former British Prime Minister Theresa May made news when she appointed a "loneliness minister" in the UK, after a study in which 9 million Brits, (nearly twenty percent of the population), were identified as lonely. In her statement, she said: "For far too many people, loneliness is the sad reality of modern life."

But this isn't just a British problem. Back in the U.S., rates of loneliness have doubled since the 1980s. In 1984, the average American had three confidants; a recent report finds that twenty-five percent now have zero.

The Western world has been suffering from detachment disorder and loneliness for longer than you or I have been alive. It's killing us in every way. If we want our communities to flourish and the Church to thrive, it will take leaders and churches intentionally, relentlessly and lovingly coming together!

Why don't we have more growing, reproducing churches? Why in the Western world is there not one healthy example of movement in the body of Christ? Why aren't there more Level 5 multiplying churches? Because we are not doing this together!

We are better together![21]

BETTER TOGETHER

"Over time, every local church that gets connected to a network naturally becomes more kingdom-minded. We begin dreaming about how to plant more churches together. Our church often celebrates great things happening within the other churches in our network and prays for churches facing difficulties." —**Anthony Cozzello, Indiana NewThing Network**

The Good News & Bad News of Level 5 Churches

For the last several years at Exponential, we have challenged church leaders, driving home this message that for us to accomplish the mission of Jesus we had to move the needle on the number of reproducing and multiplying churches. Like I told you earlier, we had done the homework and knew that approximately four percent of all churches fell into the categories of Level 4 (reproducing) and Level 5 (multiplying). The Exponential community took on that challenge and at the most recent conference, I had the privilege of reporting the good news from LifeWay Research that the needle had, in fact, moved from four percent to seven percent of reproducing churches—representing an increase of 10,000 churches that plant churches. That was really good news!

The bad news was that there was no measurable gain in the number of Level 5 churches. Why? Why are there more Level 4 reproducing churches but not more Level 5 multiplying churches? Let me offer you two reasons:

1. First, our churches in the West are not designed around forms that allow for rapid reproduction. Most of our churches are started with a "launch large" strategy that requires significant funding and full-time staff. These churches can be effective in growing and reproducing but to expect them to become Level 5 multiplying churches would mean morphing into some other form that can rapidly reproduce and thus multiply.
2. Second, and this speaks to the big idea of this chapter, our churches in the West are like the people who make them up—independent and autonomous. Like in the story of young Daniel, our churches suffer from "detachment disorder." They have not been challenged with the importance of the Great Collaboration. They don't understand the value of networks or how to form networks. They don't have the skills of collaborative leadership. They might conceptually believe they are better together, but they don't know how to do it and they don't know anyone who has done it.

That's why we have to not only take seriously the Great Commission and the Great Commandment but also the Great Collaboration. There are too many leaders who are like I was—dreaming a big dream, but thinking they have to do it on their own. In the same way, I came to realize that if I was going to see 200 churches planted all over Chicagoland, the better way to go about it was through a network than on my own. We need key apostolic leaders to have that same awakening! The big dream of a movement of multiplying churches in the Western world is best accomplished through four to five churches coming together to form networks.

If we want our communities to flourish and the Church to thrive, it will take leaders and churches intentionally, relentlessly and lovingly coming together!

Answering Jesus' Prayer

Jesus knew we would face this challenge. It's comforting knowing that He anticipated this very moment in time. It was after He prayed for His disciples that He prayed for you and me: *My prayer is not for them alone* (His disciples). *I pray also for those who will believe in me through their message* (us), *that all of them may be one, Father, just as you are in me and I am in you. May they also be in us so that the world may believe that you have sent me. I have given them the glory that you gave me, that they may be one as we are one—I in them and you in me—so that they may be brought to complete unity. Then the world will know that you sent me and have loved them even as you have loved me* (John 17:20-23, emphasis mine).

Jesus prayed that we would have the courage to do the very things we have been talking about in this book. He prayed that all who believe in Him would also come together as one. In the same way that the Father, Son and the Holy Spirit are one and in the beginning created the world together, God wants us to be one. He wants to use us to restore the world back to what He created in the beginning! That will only happen when we come together!

We can be the answer to Jesus' prayer. You can be the answer to Jesus' prayer in John 17. I can be the answer to Jesus' prayer. We have the opportunity to be the generation that comes together and leads His movement of redemption and love to a lost and lonely world. If we are one, the world will know that God is one and they will be won!

BETTER TOGETHER

"Scripture shows us the church always collaborated, showing scandalous love to others. The result was an unstoppable movement of dynamic church planting. Through our multiethnic and multi-denominational network, we are seeing the fullness of unity in our cities and the joy of the gospel in our churches." —**Oscar Leiva, Chicago NewThing Network**

Glimpses of Jesus' Prayer Being Answered

It was a Monday night in a London pub in the Spitalfields neighborhood where I got a glimpse of Jesus' prayer being answered. We had assembled leaders from all over the globe to pray and plan about how to plant 10,000 churches; see 10,000 churches commit to ongoing multiplication; and how we could do this in all 196 countries of the world.

While our dream was big and bold, it was not nearly as impressive as what I saw in the room. In that room were men and women; people of every color and hue; leaders from all over the world. The program had ended hours before, and now they were enjoying each other as friends. I saw the Filipinos hanging out with the Europeans. The Africans were laughing with some of the Americans. The Aussies were swapping stories with leaders from India. They were all gathered for one purpose—the mission of Jesus. It was the Great Collaboration. It was the answer to Jesus' prayer.

As I was finishing this chapter, I got an email from Oscar Leiva, my Chicago church planting network leader, reminding me that we were meeting at a church on Chicago's South Side next week. Oscar lives in the Pilsen neighborhood of Chicago, and I live out in the suburbs. Oscar is Hispanic, and I'm ninety-three percent English. Oscar leads a church that's Reformed in their theology, and I lean more Armenian. He's complementarian, and I'm egalitarian. Oscar and I have a lot of differences; but we both call Jesus Lord and are both committed to planting new churches together. I believe our growing friendship is an answer to Jesus' prayer.

We have the opportunity to be the generation that comes together and leads His movement of redemption and love to a lost and lonely world.

Will You Be the Answer to Jesus' Prayer?

How about you? Will you commit to being the answer to Jesus' prayer? It will require that you choose God's kingdom over your own castle. It will mean that as a leader, you make a decision to be a hero maker and not be the hero. It will mean having a circle that is big enough to include people who call Jesus Lord and small enough to focus on the mission of Jesus.

We can answer Jesus' prayer. You can. I can.

How? Together. We are always better together!

Changing the world is more than any one of us can do—*but* it's not more than all of us can do together.

We are better together!

Afterword

I have the privilege of writing to you after you've read this important book. I'm so thankful that my friends, Dave Ferguson and Patrick O'Connell, have caught the vision of the extraordinary potential that networks hold for multiplying churches and carrying out the Jesus mission.

By now, you realize that we should never underestimate the power of networking. This is one of the most important lessons I've learned in my years of church planting. Early on, as I started a church planting movement in my home country of India, God impressed upon my heart the significance of multiplying networks and consistently nurturing them. A quarter of a century later, we're seeing the results and reaping an amazing kingdom harvest. Since 1948, we have multiplied thousands of churches and networks throughout our country of 65 million Christians. Praise God!

"Together" is not just a buzzword for us. Rather, it is the essence of the Christian faith and the foundation of the Church. Dave and Patrick remind us that God the Father created the world together with His son and the Spirit. And that Jesus prayed for His disciples to be together in unity and work together (John 17:21). Today, He is calling His people—you and me— to the same standard. He's working together with His people as we establish and extend His kingdom.

Regardless of where it happens in the world, kingdom expansion is never the accomplishment of a single individual. It cannot happen that way, and Scripture repeatedly shows us it was never meant to be that way. Only together with God and the indwelling presence and power of His Spirit will we see His kingdom grow—in collaboration with individuals and teams who are graced with a variety of ministry gifts.

So now the question is: What will you do with what you've learned from this book? Will you file it away, patting yourself on the back for finishing a book about kingdom multiplication? Will you write a Twitter or blog post about it and call it good? Or will you start to make a list of faith leaders around you, praying fervently over each name that will potentially be part of the network you start? Will you identify four to five churches that have the same passions for advancing the kingdom through church planting?

I hope this won't just be another book you read or tweet about. For your sake and the sake of the leaders you'll be on this faith adventure with—and for the sake of the thousands of people who will meet Jesus in one of the churches planted by the network you join or lead. This is eternity-changing stuff that Dave and Patrick are inviting you into— it's time to pay close attention to their prophetic call.

It's time to see for yourself that we are better together.

—Sam Stephens, President of the India Gospel League

Together Discussion Guide

To help you go deeper with your circle of friends on mission, we've put together this discussion guide for each chapter. We've designed these questions to help you and your team collaborate!

Chapter 1: Better Together

OPEN

1. Think of a time someone helped you do more or achieve more than you could on your own and share your story.
2. Do you get energy from being with others or from being alone?
3. Why do you think isolation and loneliness are so detrimental to us spiritually, emotionally and even physically?

DIG

1. Read Genesis 2:18. What do you think God had in mind when He said, "man should not be alone"?
2. In Matthew 18:20, Jesus promises to be present when two or three are gathered together in His name. What does this passage tell us about being together?
3. Have you ever thought about the fact that the lack of being together is killing the body of Christ? What are some signs this is happening?

REFLECT

1. Do you agree with our big idea that we are better together? Why or why not?

2. What are some reasons many leaders try to go it alone?

3. What are some specific ways being in community with others helps us thrive as individuals?

Chapter 2: What's Missing From the Jesus Mission?

OPEN

1. Do you like puzzles? Why or why not?

2. Have you ever been frustrated by an incomplete project? What was happening? Why were you frustrated?

3. When you hear the phrase "the Jesus mission," what comes to mind? How would you explain the Jesus mission to someone in a few sentences?

DIG

1. Jesus issues the Great Commission in Matthew 28:16-20. Read the passage and identify the specific things Jesus asks His followers to do. In what way is your church engaged with this command to "Go"?

2. Mark records the Great Commandment—to love God and love others (Mark 12:28-34). Read the passage and describe what it looks like for your church to "go in love."

3. Read John 17:20-23. What does Jesus specifically say about unity and mission? Explain in your own words how collaboration with other leaders and churches for the purpose of planting churches reflects Jesus' commands.

REFLECT

1. We've created a Venn diagram illustrating how these elements (Go, Love, Together) carry out the Jesus mission. Summarize in a few sentences why we need each of these elements.

2. Do you think church planting is the best way to reach new people with the gospel of Jesus? Why or why not?

3. Do you agree that we are missing out on greater collaboration? Why or why not?

4. Would you say that collaboration is the missing piece for true kingdom movement? Or is there something else preventing movement?

5. What does the word "network" mean to you?

6. Does your church struggle when you attempt to collaborate with other churches? If so, what are some of the common patterns you've observed?

7. Sam Stephens, leader of India Gospel League, says, *Churches working together in networks are the backbone of movement.* What do you take away from Sam's insight? Do you agree with him?

Chapter 3: Together With God

OPEN

1. Who are your closest relationships in life? How did these relationships begin? When did you become close?

2. Describe a time when you were excluded from community. What happened? How did it make you feel?

3. Describe a time when someone took credit for something they didn't do? How did it make you feel?

DIG

1. Read Genesis 1:1-3. What do these verses tell us about God? How is the story of creation relevant to this "better together" conversation?

2. Read John 1:1-14. What does John tell us about the relationship between Jesus, God and the Holy Spirit?

3. How is this relationship relevant to the Jesus mission?

REFLECT

1. How would you explain to someone that God is relational? What does this mean to have a relational God?
2. How does the picture I describe of us dancing with Jesus help you understand your own relationship with Him?
3. Take a close look at the painting in chapter 3. What does it look like for you to "point to Jesus every day"?
4. Are you building a castle or the kingdom? Think hard. What evidence could you show either way?

Chapter 4: Together as a Family

OPEN

1. What are the best things your family gave you? What are the worst?
2. How does the story of Talia make you feel? How does your own origin story compare?
3. What does it look like for your family to win?

DIG

1. Read Matthew 22:37-40. What does it mean to love God and love others?
2. Where are you succeeding in the Great Commandment as it relates to your family?
3. Where are you struggling with it in your family?

REFLECT

1. I identified four factors for being a "together" family: God, marriage, identity and time. How are each of these factors functioning in your family?
2. What role does your family play in the Jesus mission?
3. Do you agree that family is mission critical? Why or why not?

Chapter 5: Together as a Team

OPEN

1. Describe a time in your life when you were part of a team.
2. What was the best part of that experience?
3. Now describe a time in your life when you tried to go it alone. What was the result?

DIG

1. Read Acts 2:42-47. What did the early church do together that your team is doing or not doing? What can you do to better align your team with the practices Luke identifies?
2. Read 1 Corinthians 12:12-30. To what does Paul compare the body of Christ? Why do you think he uses this metaphor?
3. Read 1 Corinthians 12:27. What does Paul say about the part you, your team and your church play in the Jesus mission?

REFLECT

1. Review the 10 benefits of teamwork with your team. Which ones does your team struggle with? Why? Which ones do you excel in? Why?
2. Do you agree that our default is to "go it alone"?' Why or why not?
3. When have you seen this idea of being a team centered on a cause? Was community the result? Why or why not?

Chapter 6: Together as a Church

OPEN

1. If you grew up in going to church describe that church. If you did not, describe your impression of church at that time..
2. What about the local church inspires you? What challenges you?

3. How do you feel after reading the story of Dr. Craddock and the local church? Why?
4. Have you ever experienced disunity in the local church? Explain.

DIG

1. Read 1 Corinthians 12:12-31. How does this passage inform, challenge or affirm your understanding of the local church?
2. Read Matthew 18:15-20. Now read Matthew 18:20 thinking about the context. What does Jesus say about the Church? How does this inform your understanding of the Church?

REFLECT

1. Read the questions on pages 93-94 regarding the minimum ecclesiology of the church. What are your answers to these questions? Explain why you've answered them that way.
2. Why is it essential that we are 'together' as the church? How will you apply this in your context?
3. Do you agree with Dave's leadership axiom: *lead at the smallest level and the largest level of your leadership capacity?* Why or why not?

Chapter 7: The Value of Networks

OPEN

1. Describe the neighborhood where you grew up? Did the kids in the neighborhood play together? If so, what did you play?
2. Do you work better in big groups, small groups, or alone?
3. Describe a time when God called you to do something that truly challenged you. How did you feel?

DIG

1. Read Romans 16. Now think about how we've defined networks. Would you agree that Paul describes a network in this chapter? Why or why not?

2. How does the story of network multiplication in Albania help illustrate the power of networks? Does this story inspire you or seem impossible? How does it help you think about your group or network?

3. What is your big dream? Have you given serious prayer and consideration to what it takes to accomplish it? How could others help you accomplish that dream?

REFLECT

1. Review the "5 Benefits of a Network" section. Which benefit is most appealing to you? Why?

2. What other benefits would you have included in this list? Explain.

3. If this list was "5 Challenges of Joining or Leading a Network," what would that look like for you?

Chapter 8: 10 Network Models

OPEN

1. Review the 10 models of networks. Why do you think there are so many different kinds of networks?

2. What has been your experience with networks? Explain.

3. Why have you chosen (or not chosen) to be part of a network at this time? Explain.

DIG

1. Read Jesus' vision for the church in Acts 1:8. If this is Jesus vision for how the church could go to the ends of the earth, how are networks a means for realizing that vision?

2. Is there a model of a church network that we haven't included in this list? Explain.

REFLECT

1. Which of these network models most appeals to you? Why?

2. If you are not in a network, which one of these will you join? Why?

3. What is your next step in making that happen?

Chapter 9: 7 Questions Before Starting A Network

OPEN

1. Children are notorious for being curious and asking lots of questions. What were areas of curiosity for you when you were growing up?

2. Why is it essential for leaders to ask the right questions? How would you rate yourself in this area?

3. What kind of questions do you ask before you start something new? Which questions would you add?

DIG

1. Read II Timothy 2:2. How many generations of multiplication did Paul challenge his apprentice Timothy to work towards? How could Paul's challenge be understood as a means for starting a network?

2. What are good reasons to start a network? What are bad reasons to start a network?

3. Review the first of the seven questions in this chapter. Where do you see God at work in your context? How can networks be part of it?

4. Define the word 'apostolic.' How has your understanding of apostolic leadership changed as a result of reading this book?

5. Why are relational rhythms essential in a network? Explain.

REFLECT

1. Prayerfully read all seven questions in this chapter and answer them. Share your answers with your team.

2. What is the big dream God is birthing in you? How can a network help you achieve God's dream?

Chapter 10: We Are the Answer to Jesus' Prayer

OPEN

1. Tell about a time in your childhood when you felt lonely. What happened?
2. Did that experience cause you to withdraw or reach out?
3. When did you last feel really lonely?

DIG

1. Read John 17: 20-23. Have you ever thought of yourself as the answer to Jesus' prayer? How does that make you feel?
2. Do you agree that the church in the West is suffering from "detachment disorder"? Why or why not?
3. Why do you think we're not seeing Level 5 multiplying churches?
4. How does being independent hinder the Jesus mission?

REFLECT

1. What are the specific gifts God has given you and your church?
2. How can you leverage those gifts to be an answer to Jesus' prayer in John 17?
3. What will you do differently now that you understand Jesus' Great Collaboration in John 17?

How to Start a Citywide Network

More Than BBQ in Kansas City

Kansas City is noted for its fantastic barbecue. But there is more going on in Kansas City than just great barbecue. There is a thriving church planting movement in that city led by my friends, Troy McMahon and Dan Southerland. Dan and Troy have developed a highly relational approach to expanding their circle. Their relational approach has been the catalyst for lots of new churches planted in Kansas City and has helped many of us think about how we can plant churches together.

1. Pray for your city.
2. Dream big.
3. Find others who share your dream.
4. Plant one church as a group—but plant it well.
5. Start gathering and coaching church planters.
6. Share your specific vision for the city.
7. Invite them to get in on what God is doing in the city.
8. Pool resources.
9. Give birth to another network.
10. GIVE GOD ALL THE CREDIT.

We call this process expanding your circle. The bigger your circle, the more opportunities you will have to partner with other like-minded leaders. Circles are better than rows because circles expand. And this is one of the ways we grow the kingdom.

APPENDIX 2

My Reproducing Plan (MRP)

At NewThing, we are committed to catalyzing movements of reproducing churches. This means each of us must be intentional about reproducing. We've developed this document to help you plan and commit to your unique reproducing plan. Complete this plan with your team and whoever else you need to help keep you accountable to the plan of reproducing. In the context of a movement and network, this becomes an invaluable tool.

MY REPRODUCING PLAN

Name: _____ Church/Site: _____ Year: _____

My Network is: _____ My Movement is: _____

Introduction

At NewThing we are committed to catalyzing movements of reproducing churches. This means each of us must be intentional about reproducing. We've developed this document to help you plan and commit to your unique reproducing plan. Complete this plan with your team and whoever else you need so that you remain accountable to reproducing. File this plan with your annual MOU.

My Reproducing Goals *(State in one sentence your goal in each of the following)*

My plan to reproduce a service(s) or gathering(s) in the next 12 months:

_____

My plan to reproduce a church in the next 12 months:

_____

My plan to reproduce a site/campus or missional communities in the next 12 months:

_____

My plan to reproduce and release leadership residents in the next 12 months:

_____

Identify any other reproducing initiatives you are going to undertake this year.

_____

The Present State of my church

_____ # of services/gatherings

_____ # of sites/campuses

_____ # of churches planted

_____ # of leadership residents

Future State of my church

_____ # of services/gatherings

_____ # of sites/campuses

_____ # of churches planted

_____ # of leadership residents

Identifying a Person of Peace / Apostolic Leader

When searching for other leaders for partnership, we have found this checklist helpful in finding a Person of Peace. A Person of Peace has teachability, spiritual velocity and relational intelligence. Here are some specific ways to gauge all three areas.

Teachability: In humility, a Person of Peace:

- receives input well: They ask, "What can I learn from this person?" not just, "What can I teach this person?"
- displays high levels of maturity
- confesses areas that need growth/improvement
- knows they aren't the experts at everything.

In short, the kind of leader needed to start a movement is:1) open to the input of others; 2) willing to apply that input; and over time 3) becomes an even more effective leader (Phil. 2:1-11, Matt 18:15-20, Prov. 12:1).

Spiritual Velocity: With a white-hot faith, a Person of Peace:

- asks, "How can I trust Jesus for the impossible?" not just, "How can I do something great?"
- has kingdom vision: They ask, "How can I multiply in God's kingdom?" not just, "How can I grow my church?"
- Is about church planting: They ask, "How can we plant churches that plant churches?" not just, "How can I plant a church?"
- trusts God with the unimaginable (Luke 2:52, Matt 25:14-20, Eph. 3:20).

Relational Intelligence.: With a keen awareness of people and their gifts, a Person of Peace:

- has strong networks/relational equity
- is self-aware and knows their own strengths and challenges. They ask, "How can I find my entire identity in Christ?" not "How can I find significance in a title or the size of my workload?"
- are relevant to culture: They ask, "How can my people culturally grow in their capacity and what can we create?" not, "What can you give to us to use?"

Someone with high relational intelligence has the ability to pull many people towards the momentum of what God is doing (Prov. 29:11, Prov. 12:18, Prov 13:20).

APPENDIX 4

History of Exponential Frameworks

As Exponential kicks off our 2020 theme, "Together: Pursuing the Great Collaboration," we're continuing the multiplication conversation, turning our attention to what we believe is the missing piece to a church multiplication movement in the West.

With no multiplication movements in the United States, we obviously have a leadership problem and a scorecard problem. We also have a unity problem. Church leaders are going it alone as they start new churches instead of working together. We desperately need Level 5 leaders to emerge who will intentionally come together to catalyze movements of Level 5 multiplying churches.

If we're going to make a difference and move the multiplication needle from now 7 percent of U.S. churches ever reproducing (Level 4) to a tipping point of greater than 16 percent (resulting in tens of thousands of eternities changed), we need to start with a new scorecard and paradigm for success—and that change must start in the heart and practices of leaders who recognize the truth that the mission of God won't be fulfilled by a few churches or dynamic leaders—but rather, hundreds of thousands of churches coming alongside each other to flood the fullness of Jesus into every corner of society.

Since Exponential's launch in 2006, we have come alongside church leaders to inspire, challenge and equip them to multiply disciple makers. We are a community of activists who believes that church multiplication is the best way to carry out Jesus' Great Commission and expand God's Kingdom. We dream of movements of Level 5 multipliers mobilized with new scorecards, new values, and new mindsets into every corner of society.

Since 2014 with Exponential's release of the book *Spark*, followed the next year with the watershed *Becoming a Level 5 Multiplying Church* and more than 80 to date, Exponential has introduced language, practices and assessment tools that have shaped and stewarded the multiplication conversation. Below we look at some of the key truths and concepts:

Multiplication has three critical dimensions: biblical
disciple making; a capacity for disciple making; and the mobilization of disciples and churches (more about mobilization below). Without healthy, biblical disciple making that leads to true heart transformation and deeper surrender to Jesus as Lord, we won't have multiplication that advances the Kingdom. Jesus gave us a clear, compelling, and primary cause—intended to tie together all of our worldly efforts for good.

As critical as disciple making is to multiplication, on its own it does not guarantee multiplication. We must also be responsible for building the infrastructure or capacity necessary to expand and support our church's disciple-making context.

By making biblical disciples that make disciples and plant churches that plant churches, we become more effective at carrying the fullness of Jesus into every corner of our communities, ultimately sending disciples to go and multiply new churches that create even greater capacity for healthy Kingdom growth. Disciples who make disciples the way Jesus did are the fuel of multiplication movements.

Every foundation of a powerfully aligned culture is built on three common elements:

- a unique and distinctive set of core values;
- a unique language and narrative that continually celebrates and communicates those values;
- clear expectations, practices and behaviors that bring those values to life in tangible ways for people.

When a church has strong alignment and synergy between these three elements, they start to create a specific culture. Missing just one of the three elements will sabotage your multiplication vision.

We can assess our church by looking at five levels or cultures of multiplication.

In *Becoming a Level 5 Multiplying Church*, Exponential introduced what has become known worldwide as the "Becoming 5" framework—created to help church leaders determine where they are and where they want to go. Ultimately, these multiplication levels help answer the questions, "Where are we now," and "How can we know if we're on the right track?"

The five levels include:

1. subtraction (attendance is decreasing; the leader has a scarcity mindset);
2. plateaued (attendance is not growing; leaders are between a scarcity and growth mindset);
3. addition (attendance is growing by addition; leaders are in a growth mindset)

4. reproducing (churches are reproducing programmatically; leaders
   are between a growth and multiplication mindset);

5. multiplying (the church is rapidly multiplying as a normal and
   regular part of their existence; leaders have a multiplication mindset
   and see their church through a Kingdom lens).

Churches with a multiplication culture have broken free from the
bondage of Level 3 addition thinking and have put practices in place
that close the gap between multiplication behaviors and aspirations.
They are led by courageous leaders who are more burdened by building
Kingdom capacity than local church capacity.

*To read full lists of characteristics for each multiplication level, see
Appendix A in the free eBook* Multipliers, *available via exponential.org.*

Level 5 multiplication comes through both addition and multiplication.

In the context of God's command, the
increase rests on our understanding of addition. Second, it's also
reasonable for us to conclude that the family unit was God's design
and plan for populating the earth. The family unit provides the
mechanism for "increase" through reproduction and the union of a
husband and wife.

We don't have to look any farther that Genesis to see God's design for
His people and His Church. God didn't say to Noah, "I will give you
6,000 years of life to grow one huge family with billions of children."
Instead, God established a micro or local strategy via the family where
children would be "added" to individual families. Those children
would develop, mature, and eventually be released and sent to establish
families of their own. From one family to three to nine to twenty-
seven to eighty and beyond.

The micro or local strategy for increase is addition within the family
unit. The macro strategy for increase is multiplication of families to

the ends of the earth. Each multiplication of a family provides a new context for the addition of individuals who can then become the fuel for additional new families in the future.

This is addition AND multiplication the way God naturally designed it— the way the church is intended to function. Unfortunately, our accumulation growth strategies and scorecards get in the way. Most churches behave as if they must make the biggest impact possible through addition and accumulation in a single, prolonged generation, never releasing and sending children to start additional churches.

The bottom line is that in North America, we're facing an epidemic of addition lust. Our addition-focused scorecards are holding us back from becoming leaders who work together to multiply disciples that birth new communities of faith. Our current scorecard stands in the way of Level 5 multiplication. Most churches behave as if they must make the biggest impact possible through addition and accumulation in a single, prolonged generation, never releasing and sending children to start additional churches. Multiplication spreads far and wide while addition accumulates tall and narrow.

As disciples, we have a dual calling. In 2019, Exponential took a deep dive into what it means to be "called." In many ways, this multiplication conversation is anchored by our biblical calling: We are to be and make disciples wherever we are. Throughout all time, all Christians, everywhere, have shared a primary or common calling that unites us through a common cause and mission.

We also have a secondary or unique calling that God has given us to fulfill our primary calling of disciple making. Exponential introduced the BE-DO-GO matrix to help leaders understand their unique calling and then, in turn, to come alongside others in their churches in the same way. Our personal sweet spot has three elements:

BE: Who am I created you to *be*? (design)
DO: What am I created to *do*? (purpose)
GO: Where am I created to *go*? (position)

When we're in our sweet spot, all three of these elements align. We are *who* we were uniquely created to *be*, doing *what* we were uniquely created to *do*, in the context of *where* we are uniquely created to *go*.

As we mobilize God's people in ways that equip and empower them to pursue their unique calling to make disciples, we will mobilize an army of Christ followers who will change the world as they simultaneously live out their secondary callings aligned with their primary calling. Multiplication begins and ends with obedient leaders that focus on making disciple makers *and* releasing them into the world!

Mobilization is a biblical command. The third dimension in healthy Kingdom multiplication is actually a command from Jesus: "As the Father has sent me, even so I am sending you" (John 20:21). It's easy to miss the power of Jesus' words in this single verse— Jesus, the sent one, revealing to His followers an even bigger calling than they'd first understood. The question is not, *are we sent* but rather *to where and to whom are we sent?* For most of us, the answer lies directly in the mission field already embedded in our lives.

The first two dimensions of multiplication—disciple making and building capacity for disciple making—are not enough to fulfill Jesus' command to "go." We must also mobilize disciples to carry the fullness of Jesus into every corner of society as they make disciples. We must have a culture of empowerment where the fruit of mature disciple making is disciples who go.

But mobilization gives us two tensions to manage. Scripture calls us to "live in common" as a family of believers via the church community and to simultaneously "live deployed" as missionaries in our unique corners of society. Most churches don't focus on "living deployed" practices like helping people understand their unique personal calling; equipping them to be missionaries; and helping them claim a mission field in their unique corner of society.

When it comes to mobilization, you can put churches into one of three categories, based on their underlying motives for mobilization:

1. Most churches focus on mobilizing **volunteers** to fill the service opportunities inside the church.
2. Some churches focus on mobilizing **leaders** to help scale the addition (and sometimes multiplication) capacity of the church. In most cases, leadership development systems and pipelines are the next natural progression of building addition capacity. Leadership development is an essential element for both addition and multiplication capacity.
3. Few churches focus on mobilizing **everyday missionaries** to carry the fullness of Jesus into every crack and cranny of society. This third motivation requires a church to flip itself upside down. Instead of mobilizing volunteers to build capacity to attract, serve, and accumulate more people, this third category of churches sees developing and deploying everyday missionaries to their unique corners of society as its role. Level 5 multiplication requires this type of radical, counter-church culture commitment.

A shift from hero to hero maker is critical to multiplication.
We don't need more heroes; we need hero makers who release the potential in others by moving from being addition heroes of our story to multiplication hero makers for God's glory.

When you shift from being simply the hero of your church to helping others become the heroes, you provide the future mentors your church will need on the journey toward Level 5 multiplication. That shift can be summarized into five essential practices we see in the life and ministry of Jesus, the ultimate hero maker.

Practice 1: Multiplication thinking—a shift in thinking. We move from thinking the best way to maximize ministry is through our own efforts to understanding that it actually happens through developing the leadership of others.

Practice 2. Permission giving—a shift in seeing. We take the focus off your leadership and begin to see the leadership potential in the people all around you. Looking for and identifying leadership potential in the people around you will cause you to begin to lead with a bias to "yes" and give them permission to fully engage in the mission.

Practice 3: Disciple multiplying—a shift in sharing. We begin to share not just what we know to help others follow Jesus, but to also share our lives and invest in the development of leaders who do the same for other leaders.

Practice 4: Gift activating—a shift in blessing. Not only do we ask God to bless the gifts He has given us, but we also ask God to bless the leaders we have developed and send out at the end of their apprenticeship.

Practice 5: Kingdom building—a shift in counting. We are no longer only concerned with who's showing up at our thing; we also count who's doing God's thing! Jesus told His followers in simple terms, "Seek first the Kingdom of God." They followed this admonition, and all that mattered was that God was keeping track of how the Jesus mission was being advanced around the world.

We were created for more. The local church is probably the largest and most effective volunteer force on the planet. Down deep, we know the Church that Jesus died and rose for is designed and made for so much more! Throughout Paul's letter to the Ephesian, he lays out

God's design for His Church. Based on those six chapters, Exponential identified **six paradigm shifts** and specific moves that leaders can make to revolutionize how they mobilize people and multiply disciples who multiply disciples and plant churches that plant churches.

Shift 1 From More Effort to More Jesus (Ephesians 1): Jesus has appointed His Church to express His fullness into every sphere of society. This is our foundation for mobilizing people—equipping every disciple to grow in the Lordship of Jesus and in their ability to share the gospel where they live, work, study and play.

Shift 2 From More Volunteers to More Masterpieces (Ephesians 2) Every disciple is a unique, handcrafted-by-God vessel for expressing the fullness of Jesus. As leaders, we have a responsibility to lead our church to help every disciple investigate their personal calling that mobilizes them for a one-of-a-kind mission for more.

Shift 3: From More Guilt to More Love (Ephesians 3) God's love for us and in us is the only sufficient motivation for mobilizing others— not guilt. We're called to motivate people to serve by helping them understand how loved they are in Christ.

Shift 4: From More Hierarchy to More Missionaries (Ephesians 4) Jesus has provided the organization to unleash more—found in the five-fold gifting of APEST (apostles, prophets, evangelists, shepherds, teachers). We need to help people see the Church as Jesus does.

Shift 5: From More Programs to More Mission Fields (Ephesians 5) The people of God have already been sent and strategically placed by Jesus. And for many, those places are outside the walls of your church building.

Shift 6: From More Strategy to More Surrender (Ephesians 6) When you begin to surrender our strategies and our belief that you're building the church while others help by filling the spots you've predetermined, you begin to wage the war Christ has called us to fight.

What will it take to move the multiplication needle even farther? Exponential has focused our attention on this critical question. We believe that church multiplication is the best way to carry out Jesus' Great Commission to "make disciples to the ends of the earth."

We dream of movements characterized by disciples who make disciples who plant churches that plant churches. To that end, Exponential has stewarded the multiplication conversation through numerous resources, including live regional events, more than 90 FREE eBooks, free podcasts, online courses, multiple free online assessments and much more (find them at (find them all at https://exponential.org/).

You're now part of this ongoing multiplication conversation. Our prayer is that you'll learn from Dave and Patrick's insights and be inspired to link arms with other leaders as together we storm the gates of hell.

Acknowledgments

(Dave) Sue, thanks for everything from proofing this book to being my partner and friend from day #1 on this mission. I love you!

(Patrick) Nancy, thanks for believing in me and the mission of NewThing, to be a catalyst for movements of reproducing churches.

Lindy Lowry, thanks for your work on editing and coaching to make this book the best it could possibly be.

Pat Masek, you love this mission every bit as much as we do! Please know that this book has been directly impacted by your tireless effort.

Exponential, thank you Todd Wilson, Terri Saliba and the Exponential team for believing in collaboration and creating a platform for that to happen over and over.

About the Authors

DAVE FERGUSON is an award-winning author and founding and lead pastor of Chicago's Community Christian Church, a missional multisite community considered one of the most influential churches in America. Dave also provides visionary leadership for NewThing, an international church planting movement, and is president of the Exponential conference. Dave is married to Sue, and they have three amazing kids, Amy, Josh and Caleb.

PATRICK O'CONNELL is the Global Director of NewThing, a catalyst for movements of reproducing churches. He is passionate about helping people start new things for the kingdom. He's married to Nancy and they have three great kids. He likes to run, read and hang out with friends.

Endnotes

Foreword

1. See Alan Hirsch, *The Forgotten Ways* 2nd Edition (Grand Rapids: Brazos, 2016), pp. 242-250.

Chapter 1 | Better Together

2. Dean Ornish, *Love and Survival* (New York City: Harper, 1998), p. 29.

Chapter 2 | What's Missing From the Mission?

3. Todd Wilson, Dave Ferguson and Alan Hirsch, *Becoming a Level 5 Multiplying Church* (Chantilly, Virginia, Exponential, 2015).

Chapter 3 | Together With God

4. Brian Bloye, session at 2019 Exponential conference in Orlando.

Chapter 4 | Together As a Family

5. Geoff and Sherry Surratt, *Together* (Nashville, Tennessee, Thomas Nelson Publishers, 2018).

6. Kara Powell, "5 Ways to Kill Warmth in Your Family (and how to rebuild it)," Fuller Youth Institute study, https://fulleryouthinstitute.org/blog/warmth-in-your-family.

7. John Townsend, *Boundaries With Teens* (Grand Rapids, Michigan, Zondervan, 2012).

8. Larry and Deb Walkemeyer, *Flourish* (Chantilly, Virginia, Exponential, 2017).

Chapter 5 | Together As a Team

9. Robert Crosby, *The Teaming Church* (Nashville, Tennessee, Abingdon Press, 2012).

10. Jon R. Katzenbach and Douglas K. Smith, *The Wisdom of Teams* (New York City, HarperBusiness, 1999).

11. Patrick Lencioni, *The Five Dysfunctions of a Team* (San Francisco, Jossey-Bass, 2002).

12. Ryan T. Hartwig and Warren Bird, *Teams That Thrive* (Downers Grove, Illinois, IVP Books, 2015).

Chapter 6 | Together as a Church

13. Larry Walkemeyer, *The Mobilization Flywheel* (Chantilly, Virginia, Exponential, 2018).

14. Inc.com, https://www.inc.com/amy-morin/americas-loneliness-epidemic-is-more-lethal-than-smoking-heres-what-you-can-do-to-combat-isolation.html.

15. Dr. Chuck Wickman, *Pastors at Risk* (Morgan James Faith, 2014).

16. David Brooks, *The Second Mountain* (New York, Random House, 2019).

Chapter 7 | The Value of a Network

17. Based on an interview with Pastor Altin Kita.

Chapter 9 | 7 Questions Before Starting a Network

18. Alan Hirsch, The Forgotten Ways 2nd Edition (Grand Rapids: Brazos, 2016).

19. Roland Allen, *The Spontaneous Expansion of the Church* (CreateSpace Independent Publishing Platform, 2018).

20. David Garrison, *Church Planting Movements* (WIGTake Resources LLC, 2004).

Chapter 10 | We Are the Answer to Jesus' Prayer

21. Much of the section "The Withdrawn Western World" was adapted with permission from a July 14, 2019, sermon introduction by John Mark Comer, "Community, Part 1: Jesus' call to community" at Bridgetown Church in Portland, Oregon.